DECIDE & DELIVER

DECIDE & DELIVER

5

Steps to

Breakthrough

Performance in

Your Organization

MARCIA W. BLENKO • MICHAEL C. MANKINS • PAUL ROGERS

With John Case and Jenny Davis-Peccoud
Bain & Company

HARVARD BUSINESS REVIEW PRESS

Boston, Massachusetts

Library of Congress Cataloging-in-Publication Data

Blenko, Marcia W.
   Decide & deliver : five steps to breakthrough performance in your
organization / by Marcia W. Blenko, Michael C. Mankins, and Paul Rogers;
with John Case and Jenny Davis-Peccoud.
        p. cm.
   ISBN 978-1-4221-4757-3 (hardcover : alk. paper) 1.   Decision making.
2.   Problem solving. 3.   Organizational change. I.   Mankins, Michael C.
II.   Rogers, Paul, 1958- III.   Title.
   HD30.23.B635 2010
   658.4'03—dc22

                                                              2010001433

CONTENTS

ACKNOWLEDGMENTS

Two people above all have helped to deliver this book.

Jenny Davis-Peccoud has been tireless in her contributions to the thinking and the process that produced *Decide & Deliver*. As the director of Bain's Organization Practice day to day, she has played a crucial role in directing, analyzing, and drawing insights from the research. Without her focus, skillful project management, and good humor, three spirited and vocal authors would still be debating drafts.

John Case helped to shape the concepts and the communication of our ideas. His masterful prose has made *Decide & Deliver* considerably more readable, and his resilience and patience made the writing process a lot more fun.

Many others have contributed to this book, some in ways they may not even realize. We have had the good fortune to work closely with many client executives who know what it means to decide and deliver. Some are mentioned in these pages. Others have contributed but are not mentioned by name. We thank them all for providing us with opportunities to teach a little and learn a lot along the way.

We benefited enormously from the support and brainpower of many talented business professionals at Bain, including those who conducted the research and analysis contained in this book. Special thanks go to Susan Anderson, Cornelia De Ruiter, Anna

Dominey, Maggie Locher, Christopher Lowell, Ben Olds, Joe Rieder, Tristan Smith, and Amit Thaper.

The support and encouragement of our colleagues at Bain kept us going. We are privileged to work with people who make the time to share their views and experiences, are always willing to listen and consider new ways of thinking, and are unfailingly supportive and constructive. Particular thanks go to Jimmy Allen, Mark Gottfredson, Wendy Miller, Phil Schefter, Ingo Wagner, and Chris Zook, all of whom generously contributed their time to provide thoughtful feedback at various stages of the book's development. Many other colleagues contributed as well—to each of them, our thanks.

Richard Steele, now a partner at The Bridgespan Group, merits special mention. His collaboration on a number of articles with Michael earlier in their careers contributed to important insights in *Decide & Deliver.*

Our friends and families have contributed ideas and reactions as we worked to make our ideas practical. In particular, we thank our spouses for their patience, encouragement, and support throughout. And our children, for ensuring there was little risk of taking ourselves too seriously.

Last but not least, Melinda Merino and the team at Harvard Business Review Press have been invaluable in providing feedback, inspiration, and a guiding hand on the process.

Whatever the merits of *Decide & Deliver,* much is owed to all these people. Whatever its faults, the authors had the "D." If that seems cryptic, please read on . . .

$\begin{bmatrix} 1 \end{bmatrix}$

Decisions and Results

Trevor Gregory was frustrated. A senior executive of ABB UK, the British division of the big Zurich-based power technology and automation company, Gregory was racing to put together several critical bids for clients, including the Channel Islands electricity grid, London Underground, and National Grid. The opportunities played to all of ABB's strengths as a global engineering colossus— they required technologies, project delivery, and services from several parts of the company. Few competitors could match these soup-to-nuts offerings. The contracts would mean hundreds of millions of dollars in revenues for ABB over many years.

But instead of cruising through, Gregory was bumping up against one organizational obstacle after another. The company seemed to reinvent the process for submitting major bids every time a bid came up, even though multi-million-dollar proposals like these were regular events. Worse, each of ABB's units had its own profit targets and set its own transfer prices, including a margin acceptable to that unit. By the time a bid got through the chain of ABB units, the end price was often too high to be competitive. Gregory and other managers then faced an exasperating choice. They could go in high and lose the business. They could walk away without bidding. Or they could invest blood, sweat, and tears in trying to pull the bid together, piece by laborious piece.

These opportunities are really important, Gregory thought to himself. We've got to make them happen. But he dreaded the arduous internal negotiations required to assemble the bids. Why on earth, he wondered, didn't his company work better? Why wasn't it set up to make good decisions on a routine basis for the benefit of the whole business?

THIS BOOK IS ABOUT how to fix decision failures like the ones that plagued ABB. It's about how to create an organization that hums—one that can make and execute good decisions, faster than the competition, and without too much (or too little) time and trouble.

ABB's situation was particularly severe, as we'll see in a moment: its decision failures led it to the brink of bankruptcy. But most failures are chronic rather than acute, and they show up in many companies, not just those that are courting insolvency. The signs are familiar. Decisions take longer than they should. They are made by the wrong people or in the wrong part of the organization or with the wrong information, and so turn out badly. They aren't made well, because no one is sure who's responsible for making them, or because the organization has created structures or incentives that virtually guarantee a poor outcome. Sometimes, of course, decisions *are* made, maybe even in a timely fashion. But then they are badly executed. Or else the debate starts all over again and they are never executed at all.

No company can live up to its full potential unless it can decide and deliver. Good companies can't become great. Troubled companies can't escape mediocrity. And it isn't just financial results that suffer. Organizations that can't decide and deliver are dispiriting to their employees. From the C-suite to the front line, people feel as if they're stuck in molasses or trapped inside a *Dilbert* comic strip. Aggravations and absurdities abound. The European division of an American automaker, for example, repeatedly lagged behind competitors in bringing out new features on its cars. The reason? Marketing thought it was in charge of deciding on new features. Product development thought *it* was in charge. The two functions had different incentives—marketing's were primarily on sales, product development's on costs—and so could never agree. Every proposal had to be thrashed out in long, contentious meetings. It isn't hard to imagine how the people in these functions—indeed, pretty much everybody in the organization—felt about coming to work in the morning.

But things don't have to be that way.

For more than twenty-five years, the three of us have consulted to organizations of all sorts. Our clients have included large multinational corporations, entrepreneurial ventures, research universities, and nonprofit institutions, and we have worked with leaders at every level. Despite their differences, we noticed, all these organizations share one consistent trait: when they focus explicitly on decisions, the organizations learn how to improve their performance. As their decision making and execution get better, so do their results. They can pull themselves out of the kind of downward spiral that ABB was caught in. They can create great working environments, which in turn attract the kind of people who get things done. They build the organizational capabilities to decide and deliver time and time again, in every part of the business. That, we saw, is the key to sustainable performance.

Over time, we worked with enough organizations that we began to see how to systematize this approach to decisions and performance, how to map it out and capture it in a sequence of steps. We conducted a series of research studies to validate and extend these insights. We published many of the ideas in *Harvard Business Review* and elsewhere and then refined them in light of feedback we received from executives. (See, for example, "Who Has the D? How Clear Decision Roles Enhance Organizational Performance" and "Stop Making Plans, Start Making Decisions," both in the *Review*'s January 2006 issue.) Eventually we began to discuss writing a book about it, so that not only our clients but also other organizations could kick-start the process—so that they could understand what's involved and see how others have done it.

The volume you're holding is the result. It's for every leader—no matter his or her level in the organization, no matter the size of the group he or she runs—who wants to improve how people make and execute decisions and thereby improve results. We'll show you how to assess your decision difficulties and then how to attack them. We'll outline the steps required to build an organization that can truly decide and deliver, and we'll suggest some tools that will help you along the way. We'll tell stories of companies that have dramatically improved their decision making and execution, and we'll talk about others that are well along on the journey.

Let's begin by examining what really went on at ABB, and how the company pulled itself back from the edge.

ABB's road to success

For much of the 1990s, ABB looked like the very model of a modern corporation. Its CEO, Percy Barnevik, was hailed as a visionary. Barnevik, said management writer Tom Peters, had created "the most novel industrial-firm structure since Alfred Sloan built 'modern' GM in the 1920s."[1] ABB had some five thousand profit centers, each with its own leadership team. An intricate matrix-management system linked the profit centers to one of sixty-five business areas and to country organizations around the globe.

ABB's economic performance at first seemed to justify the accolades. Beginning in 1997, however, the company began a long downhill slide. Over the next five years, its profitability plunged, its debt skyrocketed, and the value of its shares collapsed. By late 2002, the company was literally forty minutes away from filing for bankruptcy. People throughout ABB were stunned. What on earth had happened to the company that was supposed to be the shining star of the new global economy?

In truth, ABB had a litany of problems. In 1990, it had acquired Combustion Engineering, an American company that turned out to have large potential liabilities from asbestos litigation. Later in the decade, ABB's leaders were caught up in the dot-com craze; they began channeling investment away from the company's core and into speculative ventures. ABB even became embroiled in a bitter public controversy over the pension packages of a former chairman and CEO.

Like other global companies, ABB might soon have wrestled these issues to the ground. But there was another and ultimately more devastating challenge lurking below the organizational surface. As Trevor Gregory knew, the company simply wasn't set up to make good decisions on a routine basis. It couldn't act quickly. It couldn't execute well. If you had peered deeply into its inner workings at the time, you would have seen a kind of systemic decision failure, with roadblocks and potholes dotting the organizational pathways. People were snared in traps that they couldn't escape.

The lack of good information on pricing and margins, for instance, made it impossible for managers even to know which potential contracts would offer an attractive return for ABB, let alone put together a bid. How could they possibly make good decisions about which opportunities to pursue? Overall, the company was structured into a complex labyrinth, with thousands of units operating on their own. Many of these local entities controlled factories and thus did all they could to sell the products those factories made, even if that meant discouraging customers from patronizing other ABB units. Some country managers pursued acquisitions that helped their own businesses but didn't help ABB as a whole. The thousands of profit centers at ABB may have enhanced people's feelings of ownership and accountability for individual units' performance. But the coordination and motivation required to optimize the company's overall performance was missing.

These decision failures grew more severe over time. The company made more and more acquisitions, often failing to integrate them into its matrix system. Some managers began to gripe that they had three, four, even five bosses and had to get approval for major decisions from each one. With so many decisions requiring intensive negotiations, internal politics grew bitter. No one seemed able to turn things around.

And then, at last, things began to change.

In September 2002, Jürgen Dormann took over the leadership of ABB. A former CEO of Hoechst and chairman of Aventis, he moved quickly. He sold noncore assets to raise cash. He negotiated a new credit facility. He created a trust fund to settle the asbestos claims.

Most important, he began to rebuild ABB's organization so that it could again make and execute good, speedy business decisions.

Dormann and his team restructured the company, consolidating its remaining businesses into two divisions and just twenty-eight business areas, down from sixty-five. They centralized profit-and-loss accountability. They eliminated an entire management layer, streamlining decision processes. They simplified transfer pricing and required full margin transparency. Under Dormann, ABB's market and country organizations began to operate according to what the company called demand profitability: they would henceforth focus not on what they could sell from their factories, but on what they could sell to *customers* in their areas, regardless of where in ABB the product might be made. Thanks to all these measures, managers could make decisions that benefited ABB as a whole, rather than just one part of it.

But Dormann knew that those changes by themselves wouldn't be enough. ABB also needed a strong, focused organization that helped and encouraged people to make good decisions and execute them well. It needed an environment that liberated managers and employees from the silos they had worked in, that freed them to make decisions benefiting the company as a whole. Everywhere in the organization, ABB would need individuals who were able and willing to make those decisions.

So right from the beginning, Dormann built a tight, cohesive leadership team aligned around a set of clear, well-understood goals. He pushed the organization to adopt three simple values—responsibility, respect, and determination—and sponsored discussions of what those values meant in practice. His team spelled out which decisions would be made by headquarters (relatively few) and which by the divisions and business units; executives then promoted people who were committed to the new approach and who could actually make the necessary decisions. HR director Gary Steel led an initiative for a new, frugal culture, ultimately saving the company about $1.2 billion as people began factoring cost considerations into more of their decisions. Steel also revamped ABB's incentive system, putting most managers on a bonus scheme tied to a group scorecard. That, too, prompted decisions aligned with the company's interests.

By 2007, ABB was fully back on track. It was profitable. It had cash in the bank. Its share price and market value had grown more than fivefold in the previous four years. It was hit by the economic downturn, of course, but by late 2009 was climbing back. Not surprisingly, leaders who lived through the turnaround tell the story from different angles. Steel emphasizes the culture shift; another executive talks about customer focus and leadership; a third emphasizes restructuring and operational excellence. But the theme that ran through all those changes, the thread that linked them one to another, was that all contributed to eliminating the decision barriers that had hamstrung the company. As the turnaround progressed, ABB developed a new capability—the ability to make and execute the decisions that produce great performance, day in and day out. In short, the ability to decide and deliver.

Gregory, now the U.K. and Ireland CEO for ABB, summed it up for us. "The changes we went through back then gave this business an opportunity to fly," he says. "And it has flown."

Decisions matter

ABB's experience illustrates a simple and uncontroversial premise that is the starting point for this book. Decisions matter. They are to an organization what cells are to an organism: the basic building blocks. An organization's performance relative to its competitors is no more or less than the sum of the decisions it makes and executes. Better, faster decisions and better, faster execution naturally produce better results than do poor, slow, or badly executed decisions.

That's probably obvious to any executive, and there's evidence for it all over the business world. Asahi decides to introduce new "dry beer," while market leader Kirin and other competitors remain focused on traditional products. Asahi gains significant market share and is able to compete for the number-one spot in the Japanese brewing industry. Netflix offers customers the convenience of movies by mail for one flat monthly fee. Blockbuster is slow to respond—and when it later decides to compete head-on with Netflix, Blockbuster has to play catch-up. The U.K. retailers Tesco and Sainsbury, fierce competitors, both decide to launch a line of private-label products in the 1990s. But Sainsbury's positioning is confusing and its packaging unappealing; Tesco executes better, in these and in many other areas. Tesco pulls ahead, and its shareholders are handsomely rewarded.

The connection between decisions and results is intuitive; it's also supported by data on decision effectiveness that we gathered from more than 750 companies around the world. We'll discuss the implications (and limitations) of that data in chapter 2. For now, we note just two points. First, in every industry and country we studied, there is a high correlation between an organization's decision abilities and its financial results. Good decisions, made and executed quickly and effectively, go along with good performance everywhere. Second, there's an equally strong correlation between decision effectiveness and employees' attitudes. We asked people how likely they would be to recommend their company as an employer to a friend or relative, which is one of the best ways to learn how people really feel about their organization. The scores are far higher for companies that are best at making and executing decisions.

How this book is different

Nearly everyone would accept our premise about the connection between decisions and results. But here's the rub: surprisingly few companies look systematically at what gets in the way of good decision making and execution. And few take the actions necessary to improve how they make and execute their most important decisions.

The signs of this disconnect are all around us. Most organizations, for example, have never assessed their decision capabilities. They lack a reliable way to tell how good or bad they are at decision making and execution relative to competitors and peers. Nor do they know whether they are improving their ability to decide and deliver over time. Many companies invest millions, of course, in fixing organizational issues. But without knowing whether those investments improve decision abilities, it's difficult for companies to gauge whether they are likely to generate better financial performance.

A comprehensive approach to decisions

Some companies do try to address decisions directly. But even these companies often tackle only part of the problem. For instance, they may focus only on the quality of their decisions, without worrying about how much time each one takes. Yet speed can be as important as quality in determining a company's overall decision effectiveness. Execution is equally important. Larry Bossidy, who has been CEO of both Allied Corp. and Honeywell, and coauthor Ram Charan rightly emphasize in their book on the subject that companies need processes and tools to ensure that things actually happen.[2] But a decision approach takes us a step further.

It ensures both that the decisions an organization makes are actually worth implementing and that the organization helps move every individual decision from "made" to "executed."

There's another partial approach that some companies pursue as well. They concentrate on the big, strategic decisions made in the executive suites, devoting considerable management attention to ensuring that these decisions are made well. They pay far less attention to improving the day-to-day operating decisions made by middle managers and frontline workers. Yet some decisions in the latter category may be just as important to success, perhaps even more so. Sales reps' decisions about discounts and terms, marketing managers' decisions about promotions and ad placements, procurement specialists' decisions about how much to pay for parts and components—for some companies, getting all these decisions right can add hundreds of millions of dollars to the bottom line.

So we want to introduce a new way of thinking. We want to look squarely at decisions, and we want to look at every element of decision effectiveness, including execution. We want to help you identify your organization's most important decisions wherever they may be, assess them, and make them more effective from start to finish.

Organizations, not just individuals

This book is also different in another way. It looks not just at how well *individuals* make and execute decisions, but also at how much *organizations* help or hinder people in doing so.

Much has been written on decisions in recent years. Current research has shed light on how biases in the human brain affect the way an individual makes choices. Malcolm Gladwell's *Blink* and Dan Ariely's *Predictably Irrational*, for example, have helped many people understand these built-in biases.[3] Other research has examined how teams can make better decisions by avoiding groupthink and other impediments and by incorporating a diversity of views that can then be vigorously debated. And several recent books have described new methods and systems for improving decision processes. *Competing on Analytics*, by Thomas H. Davenport and Jeanne G. Harris, shows how companies can use sophisticated software and analytical procedures to help leaders make better decisions.[4] James Surowiecki's *Wisdom of Crowds* describes methods for tapping the collective knowledge of large groups.[5] Companies applying such methods often report significant improvements in the way they make important decisions.

Valuable as these approaches are, however, individual and team-based approaches regularly run into an insuperable barrier: the organization. After all, every decision in business is ultimately made and carried out within the context of an organization, often a large and complex one. Even if individuals and teams have honed their decisions skills and developed innovative decision processes, the organization can stop people in their tracks. Consider ABB. The managers of each unit Trevor Gregory had to deal with may have been highly skilled decision makers. But those managers still made decisions designed to maximize their own units' profitability, because of flawed transfer-pricing information. The decisions still reflected the every-unit-for-itself culture that ABB had cultivated, and they still ended up harming the company as a whole.

It isn't just seriously troubled organizations such as pre-Dormann ABB that impede good decision making and execution. Take Lafarge, the French building materials giant. Lafarge has long been a superior performer, one of the most respected companies in its industry. And when new CEO Bruno Lafont took the reins in January 2006, he mapped out an ambitious plan for growth. Implementing that plan fell to operating executives such as Gérard Kuperfarb, copresident of the company's Aggregates & Concrete Division. In the past, Kuperfarb's concrete business focused on Lafarge's traditional markets, including France, the United Kingdom, and the United States. Now it set its sights on expanding aggressively in the developing world. To get there, Kuperfarb knew, the division had to beat its principal competitors—local independent operators—by ensuring world-class execution at every site. It also had to capitalize on Lafarge's global scale by rolling out a common operating model, including, for example, new value-added products such as quick-set concrete, to all its local operations.

But Lafarge's concrete organization wasn't yet tuned to this level of performance. One problem: decision authority wasn't necessarily in the right place. In some areas of the United States, for instance, truck dispatching was handled by regional managers responsible for large geographic areas. Site managers often felt that they could make better dispatching decisions themselves because they were closer to customers and more familiar with local conditions—but they didn't have the authority to do so. A second problem: the company was organized differently from one country to another. When it came time to roll out value-added products across the entire organization, different people in each market organization were likely to have responsibility for key issues such as sales training. That didn't make for easy, seamless rollouts. Finally, Lafarge had layer upon layer of support functions—organizations within the company that were widely perceived as bureaucratic and resistant to change. All of these issues could stymie Kuperfarb's vision of global expansion.

Our message

The central message of the book is this: you can't consistently improve decision making and execution in a company without looking at the entire organizational system. You need to build an organization that supports and encourages decision making and execution rather than one that erects barriers. You need an organization that enables individuals and teams, day in and day out, to *use* the skills and procedures that make for great decisions. You also need an organization that can regularly and effectively execute those great decisions if you hope to deliver great results.

At first glance, building such an organization might seem like a tall order. You would need to reexamine the organization's structure—the first stop for many frustrated executives—to see if it facilitates good decisions. You'd want to inspect the roles involved in major decisions to be sure that they are properly defined and clear to all. You would certainly look at decision processes and the flow of information, and you would need to know whether you have people with the necessary skills and motivation in positions where they can make and carry out the important decisions. You'd also assess your performance measurements and incentives—do they help or hinder individuals' ability to make and execute good decisions, and to do so quickly? And, of course, you would scrutinize your organization's cultural norms and values, the everyday assumptions that govern how people act. Do leaders model the behaviors that reinforce good decisions? Do people in the organization emulate those leaders?

While such a holistic approach can sound daunting, it is the key to success. And decisions offer a practical point of entry to what would otherwise be a large and potentially overwhelming task. Once you shine a light directly on decisions, the organizational obstacles and bottlenecks suddenly show up in stark relief. You can see adjustments that will help you make your most important decisions better and faster. You can see what else in the organization needs to be changed to sustain good decision making and execution, and you can begin fixing that. Over time, you can embed the changes in the way the organization works. And you can gauge your progress by assessing your decision effectiveness before and after.

Lafarge's Aggregates & Concrete Division, for instance, implemented a series of measures designed to facilitate better decision making and execution. It eliminated layers and simplified reporting lines. It clarified the roles managers played in key decisions. One of the most important changes was to push many decisions out to people who could make better choices and execute them faster. Dispatch and pricing were now handled at local sites. Only a few of the critical decisions, such as geographic investment priorities and capital expenditures, remained the province of senior leaders. Thanks to such measures, the division trimmed overhead costs and improved effectiveness, raising its operating profit from 7.4 percent to 9.5 percent. It increased its share of value-added products from a very low level (except in France) to an average of about 30 percent worldwide. And it achieved its goal of expanding into developing countries, with emerging markets accounting for 50 percent of sales in 2009 compared with 10 percent five years earlier. These changes helped Lafarge weather the downturn better than many of its competitors.

Five steps to better performance

Our plan of attack for improving decision effectiveness includes the following five steps (figure 1-1). We'll devote a chapter to each.

1. *Assess your decision effectiveness—and how your organization affects it.* It's hard to improve until you know where you're strong and where you're weak. Maybe your organization typically makes good decisions, for example, but takes too long to do so. Or maybe the real bottleneck is translating decisions into action. Chapter 2 defines what we mean by decision effectiveness and describes our research into how companies can assess it. Using the information we gathered as a kind of diagnostic database,

FIGURE 1-1

Five steps to improving decision effectiveness

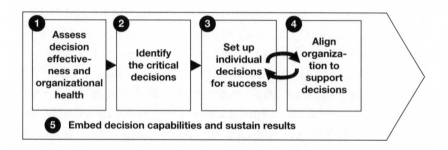

you can create a "decision scorecard" showing how you stack up against competitors on each dimension of decision making and execution. You can also develop an organizational scorecard to indicate which elements of your organization are the greatest barriers to decisions.

2. *Identify your critical decisions.* People in any large organization make millions of decisions. But in our experience, more than 80 percent of most companies' value is tied to less than 20 percent of the decisions its organization makes and executes. Since you can't focus your attention on every decision, it makes sense to concentrate on those that are most important. Some of these critical decisions are obvious—they're the major strategic choices that typically involve allocating large amounts of resources. Others are daily operational decisions that cumulatively create (or destroy) a lot of value. Chapter 3 shows you how to lay out your "decision architecture" and identify your most important decisions, those that carry the most value. It then shows you how to X-ray these critical decisions to understand the trouble spots and prepare to address them.

3. *Redesign individual critical decisions for success.* With your critical decisions identified, you can begin applying best practices to those that are most in need of improvement. Does everyone understand exactly what the decision is? Are all the roles clear to everybody? Is the necessary information available at the right time, and are the procedures for decision making and execution well defined and well understood? Does everyone know the timetable? It's often amazing how much progress organizations can make simply by applying time-tested decision tools and techniques to their most important decisions. Chapter 4 shows how.

4. *Ensure that the organization enables and reinforces great decision making and execution.* Fixing individual

decisions is a start. But it rarely solves the whole problem, because the real trouble often lies outside the mechanics of any one decision. Sometimes, the organizational structure makes it impossible for decision makers to act quickly. Sometimes, the style of decision making slows things down—too great an emphasis on consensus, say. View the entire organization through the lens of your critical decisions, as we do in chapter 5, and you'll see barriers and potholes that you might otherwise have missed. Then you can eliminate them, one by one.

5. *Embed the changes in everyday practice.* Once on the path to decision effectiveness, companies find all sorts of ways to make the changes stick, as we'll see in chapter 6. They celebrate good decisions and reward the people responsible. They build a common vocabulary of decision effectiveness. They create tools for redesigning individual decisions and embed new decision capabilities through coaching and training. They stay focused on the decisions that carry the greatest value, which means that the new approaches will have a significant impact. Not surprisingly, these companies closely track and monitor their performance—and they continue to adjust the organization so that it reinforces good decision making and execution over time.

Implementing these five steps may be a big job or a modest one, depending on your organization's situation. But we don't recommend omitting any one of the five. Each is essential to success.

The payoff

In many years of work with clients, we have noticed that the highest-performing organizations have a distinctive look and feel about them. It's true of present-day ABB, Lafarge's Aggregates & Concrete Division, and many others that we will describe in this book. The people in these organizations—and it doesn't matter where they sit—*know* how to decide and deliver. They intuitively understand which decisions are most important. Executives and frontline workers share a common vocabulary and set of expectations about how to make and execute those decisions. People know how to collaborate across the organization to make decisions that benefit the business, and they are able to respond quickly and flexibly to changing circumstances. If some element of the organization—its incentives, its processes, or something else—is getting in the way, the leaders work hard to change that element. The result is continuous improvement, but not in the usual sense of the term. These companies continuously improve their decision effectiveness and thus their performance.

Decision effectiveness, in short, is a path to a better organization, one that accomplishes what it sets out to do and that liberates rather than oppresses the people who work for it. If your company understands which decisions are critical to its performance, if it can make them better and faster than the competition, if it can execute them more effectively, well, then we're right back where we began this chapter, with the connection between decisions and results. Making a step change in your decision capabilities should, over time, provide a sustainable competitive edge, create enormous value for shareholders, and help turn your organization into a great place to work.

[2]

Score Your Organization's Decision Abilities

Hospira, a specialty pharmaceutical and medical device company headquartered near Chicago, had a pretty good track record in the five years since it was spun off from Abbott Laboratories. Sales had grown to $3.6 billion. Its two primary product lines, generic injectables and medication management systems, were doing well. The company employed fourteen thousand people and had several major facilities in the United States and overseas. Still, CEO Chris Begley felt that Hospira had more potential than it had yet realized. In early 2009, he and his team announced an ambitious plan for growth coupled with more than $100 million in cost savings. If the plan succeeded, Hospira would join the top quartile of companies in its industry. That's where Begley felt it belonged.

But was Hospira's organization up to the challenge? Frankly, Begley wasn't sure. Decisions took longer than they should. They involved too much time and trouble. And it wasn't just the big C-suite decisions—at least Begley could intervene personally in many of those. It was all the decisions that had to be made farther down in the organization, week in and week out. Marketing brochures, for example. Hospira produced hundreds of these a year, and the process for each was painfully slow. Drafts were passed along in manila folders. Each person added his or her comments and moved them along the chain. It was never clear who had the final say. By default, it seemed to be the regulatory team, which was rigorous in ensuring that the wording complied with federal rules. But the marketing angle—did the brochure also tell a compelling sales story?—often seemed to be missing.

Begley knew, moreover, that brochures were just the tip of a decision iceberg. If the company couldn't speed up its metabolism on that kind of issue in every part of the business, could it really deliver on its aspirations to enter the top ranks?

T O   T A C K L E   Y O U R   O R G A N I Z A T I O N ' S decision challenges, you naturally have to begin by assessing its strengths and weaknesses in decision making and execution. No competent doctor prescribes medicine without conducting a thorough diagnosis of the patient's condition. So it is with organizations. Some, like ABB before Jürgen Dormann's arrival, face serious challenges across the board. Others, like Hospira, want to ensure that they're firing on all cylinders to support the next phase of growth. In either case, the first step of our five-step framework is a solid, fact-based evaluation of where your organization currently stands.

The assessment should focus on just two broad areas, decision effectiveness and organizational health:

- The *decision scorecard* tells you how well or poorly you're doing on decisions. It includes an assessment of all the elements of decision effectiveness—decision quality, speed, and so on—and allows you to benchmark performance against other organizations.

- The *organization scorecard* shows what elements of your organization may be hindering people from making good decisions quickly and implementing them effectively. It helps you home in on the barriers to better decision making and execution. You can benchmark your organization scores against others as well.

Have you ever noticed how exposing a performance gap often prods people into action? We have found over the years that these twin assessments can galvanize an organization. Managers who might have been complacent about a company's performance can suddenly see the possibilities for improvement. Leaders who sense that their organizations could be more effective but who aren't sure where to start can pinpoint the areas most in need of improvement. It's the burning-platform phenomenon: when people see the threats and the opportunities with their own eyes, they're ready to act. In a large, complex organization, that alone can be of real value.

We have developed a systematic method of making these assessments and have refined it over the years both from experience and from the research we'll describe in this chapter. We'll walk you through it here. We'll also outline precisely what we mean by decision effectiveness and describe how to measure it. All this should help you identify specific strengths and weaknesses in your organization's decision making and execution. It should also help you determine which aspects of the organization are the most likely sources of decision problems and should thus be at the top of your priority list. Later in the chapter, we'll show you how to create a quick-and-dirty assessment of your own organization, to get a preliminary sense of where things stand.

What is decision effectiveness?

You can't assess decision effectiveness until you know what it is. In our view, it has four distinct components.

Quality

One element of decision effectiveness is, obviously, decision quality—that is, whether a company makes good decisions more often than not. Contrary to what the ready-fire-aim school of management might claim, no company can generate consistently good performance without high-quality decisions.

How do you assess quality? Well, they say that hindsight gives you perfect vision, and the chief criterion for a good decision is whether in retrospect you believe you chose the right course of action. In 2000, for example, Time Warner merged with America Online in a $112 billion transaction. The combination failed to pay off, and the man who presided over it, then-CEO Jerry Levin of Time Warner, later dubbed it "the worst deal of the century."[1] So it's safe to say that the acquisition was a poor decision. Southwest Airlines decided in the early 2000s to hedge its fuel costs aggressively, effectively locking in fixed prices for much of the jet fuel it used in its operations. When petroleum prices skyrocketed in 2007, Southwest was protected against the worst of the cost increase and was one of the few airlines to remain profitable. The company's hedging decision was a clear winner.

Good decisions are based on relevant facts, not on opinions or guesswork. They assess risk as accurately as possible. They involve rigorous debate of alternatives. They take into account an organization's ability to execute. To be sure, a decision may be the best that could have been made at the time and still lead to an unfavorable outcome. Much in the world is beyond our control, after all. But a company with a robust approach to decisions should have a pretty high hit rate on quality.

Decision quality is of paramount importance in some industries. In petrochemicals, for example, the decision about when and where to build a new ethylene cracker—a multibillion-dollar investment—can have a tremendous impact on a company's long-term performance. If management chooses to build at the wrong time, in the wrong location, or with the wrong technology, the company must live with the consequences for many decades. Accordingly, companies such as The Dow Chemical Company rightly devote significant time and energy to making the best possible decisions on such matters.

But quality isn't the only thing that matters. A while ago, for example, we were talking with Bill Graber, a twenty-six-year veteran of General Electric who later became chief financial officer of McKesson, the health-care services company. Graber outlined his view of what lay behind GE's extraordinary performance during the late 1980s and 1990s. "There is this myth about GE," he said. "Many people believe that we made *better* decisions than our competitors. That's just not true. Our decisions probably weren't any better than many other companies'. What GE did do was make decisions a lot *faster* than anybody else, and once we made a decision, we *followed through* to make sure we delivered the results we were expecting. That speed and follow-through opened up a lot of opportunities for GE—opportunities that our competitors never saw, because they didn't move fast enough or act decisively enough."

Speed

As Graber suggested, how quickly an organization moves can be as important as how good its decisions are. "Fast-fashion" retailers such as Zara and Topshop make and execute decisions about in-season apparel trends much faster than mainstream retailers traditionally have done, bringing new products to the shelf in weeks rather than months. Their growth rates have been more than twice the industry average. J.P. Morgan Chase & Co. acquired Bear Stearns at what many observers felt was a bargain-basement price during the early days of the 2008 financial crisis. It was the only bank able to decide to do so in the time allowed to potential acquirers by the Federal Reserve. Of course, we aren't advocating speed for its own sake; companies sometimes move too quickly, without due consideration of risks and alternatives. Lloyds Banking Group's acquisition of HBOS during the financial downturn—also done at a breakneck pace—proved challenging to the venerable British bank and contributed to a loss of £4 billion in the first half of 2009.

What counts most isn't absolute speed, which will vary according to the business you're in and the kind of decision you're making, but speed relative to competitors. In fast-changing industries such as high technology or media, nearly every participant moves quickly. So some decisions must often be made in a matter of days or even hours. Thus, for companies like eBay or Google, it's better to get the answer half right and change things later than to push for additional analysis and miss out altogether. On the other end of the speed spectrum, pharmaceutical companies require many years to bring out a new drug. But a study of the industry concluded that drugs developed by the five fastest-moving companies, including Bayer, AstraZeneca, and Merck, earned an average of $1.1 billion *each* in incremental prescription revenue between 2000 and 2005, compared with drugs from the slowest-moving companies.[2]

Yield

Individuals often make decisions they fail to follow through on—going on a diet, for example. Organizations are no different. How many of us have worked for companies that make bold pronouncements about improving quality or customer service but then fail to implement those pronouncements? How many have seen year after year of "hockey stick" forecasts, each showing performance shooting up in future years—performance that is never realized because the company's strategy is never adequately executed? Poor execution of a decision that has been made (or a complete failure to execute, as sometimes happens) naturally undermines any virtues the decision itself might have had.

Yield—how well a company turns its decisions into action—is always critical to performance. When BP bought Amoco in 1998, for instance, the acquirer executed the merger so well that it achieved its projected $2 billion in cost savings in just one year. In some industries, execution itself is a powerful source of competitive advantage. Plenty of airlines patterned their fundamental strategy after Southwest's, only to find that they couldn't execute the strategy the way Southwest can. Few of those carriers have generated Southwest's levels of profitability over time.

What counts here, by the way, isn't just the implementation of big, strategic decisions. Performance always depends on how well middle managers and frontline employees make and execute the day-to-day decisions that they are responsible for. Nordstrom built its strong position in apparel retailing partly through its selection and presentation of appealing merchandise, reflecting the decisions of buyers and merchandisers throughout the organization, and partly through its legendary customer service. Salespeople are expected to do the right thing by every customer, whether it's accepting a return with no receipt or going the extra mile to track down a particular item. But this expectation would mean little unless it was implemented every day by the people on the floor.

Effort

There's one more element of decision effectiveness that we have encountered over and over in our work. Effort is the time, trouble, expense, and sheer emotional energy it takes to make and execute a decision. How many committees must a decision go through? How many people must sign off on it? How many analyses and reviews must be conducted before they do? How difficult is the translation of a decision into action? Decision effectiveness obviously suffers if the effort involved is greater than what the decision merits. It can also suffer if the effort involved is too little. A decision that is made too quickly and easily, without consideration of the relevant information and experience, may be plain wrong. Even if it is right, it may lack the support necessary to ensure effective implementation.

Effort is a little different from the other three elements of decision effectiveness. It's like a tax—necessary, but important to keep at an appropriate level. Effort becomes an issue only when it is substantially higher or lower than it ought to be.

Importance of all four elements

By noting that one element may be particularly important in a given industry, we don't mean to imply that people in that industry can forget about the others. On the contrary: throughout our work, we have repeatedly noted that companies scoring high on just one or two elements are at a disadvantage compared with better-rounded competitors. For example, the quality of a company's decisions always matters a lot. But no company succeeds just by making exceptionally good decisions. Conversely, no amount of speed or great execution can make up for a flawed strategy or wrong choices. Ultimately, you have to make decisions that are worth executing.

So all four elements are essential. This conclusion stems not just from our experience, but also from the research we conducted for this book.

What the research shows

The best way we know of to understand how well (or how poorly) a company makes and executes decisions is to ask the people who work there. So several years ago, we began to survey executives around the world about their organizations' performance on each of these decision elements. We had two objectives in mind. One was to add some quantitative insights to our experience. Did decision effectiveness correlate with financial results? Did companies tend to excel in one element or another, or were some companies high performers in every element? Were we right in our judgment that the latter would nearly always outperform the one-trick ponies? And what about trade-offs? Did decision speed, for instance, tend to compromise quality, or maybe yield?

Our other objective was to create a kind of diagnostic database for benchmarking purposes. Companies could use our data to see how their own performance on each of the four elements measured up against competitors and peers.

A series of studies over the years culminated in a major international survey conducted in 2008. This one covered some 760 companies worldwide. The respondents came from every managerial level, from the C-suite on down. (For more details on the survey, please see the appendix.) We asked respondents how effective their companies were overall at making and executing their most important decisions. We also asked the respondents to rate their companies on the individual elements. *In retrospect, how often does your organization make the right decision? How quickly is your organization able to make decisions—faster than competitors, slower, or about the same?* And so on. Data in hand, we combined the score on each element into one overall score on decision effectiveness. Then we assessed each company's financial performance so that we could quantify the relationship between decisions and results. This research turned up four practical conclusions, outlined in the following pages.

High decision effectiveness and great performance

The overall correlation between decision effectiveness and performance was extraordinarily strong, holding up at a 95 percent confidence level or higher for every country, industry, and company size we studied. Companies with the highest scores on decision effectiveness consistently generated higher levels of revenue growth and return on invested capital. Top-quintile companies on decisions produced an average total shareholder return about 6 percentage points higher than that of other companies.

This relationship isn't surprising, given the intuitive connection between decisions and performance. There is a risk, of course, that some of the relationship might be explained by the halo effect, common in business research: people in companies that are doing well on one parameter, say financial performance, also see themselves as doing well in other areas, in this case decisions. So we took a number of steps to counteract the halo effect and ensure the validity of our findings. Wherever possible, we asked questions that gave us quantitative answers. *What percentage of your organization's decisions turn out to be correct? How many important decisions did your organization make last year? What percentage of the time do you execute major decisions as intended?*

We also analyzed relative patterns in the data. Contrary to what we would have observed had the halo effect been significant, we found that most companies didn't score uniformly well or poorly on all four elements of decision effectiveness. Finally, we (or our Bain colleagues) were able to provide an independent view of many companies' decision-effectiveness profiles. We didn't include our own views in the data, of course, but the general similarity between company responses and our external view reassured us that our input data was reasonably good.

A multiplier effect

The research supported our view that each of the first three components of decision effectiveness—quality, speed, and yield—is itself linked to financial performance. For instance, companies that make better decisions generate significantly higher shareholder returns than the average company does over a five-year period, whatever their scores on the other elements. The same is true for speed and yield.

But the real lesson we discovered is a multiplier effect. Combine the three components into one overall score of decision effectiveness through multiplication, and you find a far tighter correlation with financial results than when you use any one element alone. In other words, any one element makes some difference, but all three together make a *lot* of difference. So executives who focus on only one are missing two-thirds of the picture. Speed and yield each matter a good deal more than most people think; in fact, they're on a par with quality in relation to a company's financial performance. High decision effectiveness and outstanding financial results require high scores on quality, speed, *and* yield.

Effort as a drag on performance

Effort wasn't as highly correlated with financial performance as the other three components. But including it allowed us to refine the assessment further. For example, it helped us differentiate between truly great companies and merely good ones. Of all the companies with high scores on quality, speed, and yield, slightly fewer than half reported effort as too high or too low. Once that "effort tax" is factored in, this group has an overall decision score only 66 percent that of the optimal-effort group's, and so these companies have to be scored as runners-up rather than winners. The runners-up, incidentally, were about equally split between too much effort and too little.

Whatever a company's score on quality, speed, and yield, inappropriate effort will drag down performance. The reasons aren't hard to understand. Decisions get bogged down if there are too many committees and too many reviews. People get fed up and go with the path of least resistance. Conversely, some companies devote too little effort to their most important decisions. They shoot from the hip, miss the target, and pay a financial penalty as a result.

Few trade-offs

Executives often ask us whether there are trade-offs between quality, speed, yield, and effort. "If we push too hard to make decisions faster, won't we end up making poorer-quality decisions?" "If we push too hard on decision quality, are we likely to miss windows of opportunity for quick action?" The concern is understandable. Resources are always limited, so you might think a company that was particularly good at one element of decisions would pay the price in other areas. And in some cases, the trade-offs are real. Many companies can (and often must) make some decisions quickly even if all the data isn't in, and can sometimes correct the decisions that turn out to be wrong. If a decision is hard to reverse, of course, it's nearly always a mistake to sacrifice decision quality for speed.

But though top performers may encounter trade-offs in any one instance, the overall picture is quite different. High scores on one element of decision effectiveness are not typically associated with low scores on the other elements. Companies that score high on speed, for example, don't automatically score low on quality or even yield. Quite the contrary: companies that make the fastest decisions are about *four times* as likely to make high-quality decisions as companies with average or low speed scores. Similar relationships hold with the other elements. The lesson for trade-offs is this: people in a top-performing organization naturally dial speed up and down, depending on the nature of a particular decision. Even so, they typically move faster than competitors on their most important decisions. Our experience with the best-performing companies has borne this out again and again.

The implications of this finding are profound. A company we worked with, for example, made relatively good decisions and executed them well. But the company's score on decision speed was far lower—a situation that executives justified by saying, "It's important for us to take our time so that everyone gets on board and we can be assured of good execution." The data suggests that tunnel vision of this sort is misguided, particularly in today's fast-changing world. If a competitor has cracked the code on all four components—if, for instance, it can make an equally good decision and engage its people without slowing the process to a crawl—then it will outperform the laggards every time.

Benchmarking decision effectiveness

Much of the value of this research lies in its use for benchmarking. The data shows where an organization is stronger and weaker than other companies. A company that's aspiring to be a top performer in its industry will almost certainly need to be a top performer in decisions.

Research conclusions: A quick summary

- **Decisions = performance.** Decision effectiveness and financial results correlate at a 95 percent confidence level or higher for every country, industry, and company size we studied. Top-quintile companies on decisions generate average total shareholder returns nearly 6 percentage points higher than those of other companies.

- **Quality, speed, and yield reinforce one another.** Each factor alone correlates with financial results. But the product of all three is a much stronger predictor of financial performance than any single element.

- **Effort is a drag.** Effort levels differentiate between truly great companies and merely good ones. Of all the companies with high scores on quality, speed, and yield, for instance, nearly half report effort as too high or too low—and this group's overall decision score is only two-thirds that of the optimal-effort group.

- **Few trade-offs.** Although it's counterintuitive, high performance on quality goes along with high performance on speed and yield, and vice versa. For instance, companies that score the highest on quality are nearly eight times as likely to execute their decisions effectively as those with average or low quality scores.

- **Room for improvement.** On a decision-effectiveness scale of 0 to 100, top-quintile companies score an average of 71. All other companies average only 28. The size of the gap may be surprising, but it is due to the multiplier effect of quality, speed, and yield on overall decision effectiveness. Stated differently, the average organization has the potential to more than double its ability to make and execute critical decisions.

Companies can benchmark each element of decision effectiveness; they can also benchmark their overall decision score. We compiled overall scores using the following method. Reflecting the multiplier effect of quality, speed, and yield, we multiplied the scores for those three components together. Then we corrected for the effort tax to get the final score. The formula looks like this:

$$\text{Decision score} = \text{Quality} \times \text{Speed} \times \text{Yield} - \text{Effort}$$

Hospira, for example, administered a survey like ours to the top three hundred people in the organization, including every function and geographical unit. When the results were in, the news wasn't nearly as good as CEO Begley had hoped. The company's decision score came out below average (around the 40th percentile)—a far cry from the top quartile to which Begley and his team aspired. Decision quality was fairly good, but speed was below average and effort was higher than it should have been. Nearly 80 percent of respondents, regardless of level or function, said decisions took too much effort. Top-level respondents actually rated speed and effort worse than did others in the organization, perhaps because these higher-level leaders were involved in thorny cross-functional or cross-unit decisions.

Begley and the team asked themselves whether, from their own experience, the scores rang true. They had to admit that the scores seemed on the mark. They thought back to the marketing brochures, for example. Clearly, those decisions, with their many manila-folder stopping points, took too long to wend their way through the system. And the need to reconcile everybody's handwritten changes meant that effort was definitely higher than it needed to be. But speed and effort weren't the only issues. The feedback from the sales organization was that the brochures weren't all that great. The company was taking too much time, devoting too much effort, and still not making the best possible decisions.

For Hospira, as for many organizations we have worked with, benchmarking was a wake-up call. Begley began to see that if Hospira could move the needle on its weakest elements, the company's whole metabolism could begin to function better. It would accelerate the journey toward top-quartile performance.

But Begley also had to ask himself what was holding things back. With the marketing brochures, it was most likely the decision process that needed fixing. But what about all the other decisions that were taking too long or requiring too much effort? Maybe talented people weren't in the right positions. Maybe the culture somehow encouraged people to act slowly. Or maybe it was something else entirely. Hospira, like any company that has assessed its decision effectiveness and found it wanting, now had to move on to the second part of the assessment: the organization.

Assessing organizational health: Where are the decision barriers?

The 2008 survey included thirty-nine questions designed to gauge specific organizational areas that we knew from experience often affect decision effectiveness. The survey offered statements on a broad range of topics and asked respondents to what extent they agreed. For example: *Individuals are clear on the roles they should play in making and executing critical decisions. People with decision authority have the skills and experience to make good decisions.* The responses to these and the thirty-seven other statements allowed us to create another scorecard for benchmarking—one that gauged each company's organizational health.

This scorecard, naturally, includes a lot of information. Organizations are complex entities, after all, and, like human beings, can come down with any number of afflictions that compromise their performance. To simplify things, we bundled the questions into ten common areas and labeled each with a medical-sounding term for poor performance. Like a bad back or a trick knee, any of these ailments can compromise your organization's overall performance:

- *Structural sclerosis.* The organization's structure gets in the way of good decision making and execution.

A rental-car company in Europe, for instance, was organized by country and so was unable to offer seamless service to the highly profitable travelers who crossed country borders.

- *Decision ambiguity.* Nobody is quite sure who should play what role in major decisions. Remember the auto company we mentioned in chapter 1? Both the marketing and the product development functions believed they had the final call on new-product features.

- *Process paralysis.* Business processes are undermined by ineffective decision processes. One pharmaceutical team worked for months to develop product-introduction recommendations, only to have steering committee members postpone the decision and request different analyses, delaying execution.

- *Data dysfunction.* The information needed to support major decisions isn't available at the right time or in the right format. So people are left trying to make decisions in the dark—or else they're swamped with more data than they can possibly decipher and use.

- *Misaligned measures.* Measures and incentives don't reinforce good decisions. Look no farther than the 2008 Wall Street debacle: many traders were rewarded for short-term decisions that hurt their companies' long-term value.

- *Blurred vision.* People throughout the organization lack a clear context for making and executing the decisions they're involved in. In military language, they don't even know what hill to take, let alone how they are expected to take it.

- *Consensus overdose.* The organization's principles for making decisions aren't effective. For example, people may spend too much time trying to get agreement. Everyone can say no, but no one can say yes.

- *Talent deficiency.* Positions with major impacts on decisions aren't held by people with the necessary experience and competencies. Some of the right people aren't even on the bus, and others are in the wrong seats.

- *Behavior breakdown.* Leaders don't walk the talk. The way they act undermines effective decision making and execution.

- *Performance anemia.* The organization's culture gets in the way of effective decisions. Maybe the culture is sluggish and apathetic—people just aren't engaged. Or maybe it's too averse to risk. Or it's too polite, and people never get into the tough debates that are essential to good decisions.

No magic bullet

Is there a direct, one-to-one relationship between any of these organizational ailments and specific decision weaknesses? That's one of the most common questions executives ask us. And indeed, it's only reasonable to hope that a company with low scores in one area of decision effectiveness could improve its performance by correcting a corresponding area of its organization.

We've looked for those magic bullets. Sadly, there seems to be no consistent relationship between a given organizational area and a specific element of decision effectiveness. Too many factors can intrude. For example, you might think that a company that makes decisions slowly could improve purely by revamping its decision processes. But what if the real trouble is the lack of clear priorities, which leads people to dither? Or what if the organization's structure is getting in the way?

In fact, the research pointed us in quite a different direction. Not only is there no magic bullet, but companies also can't expect to improve their decision effectiveness simply through superior performance in one or another organizational element. Rather, an integrated approach is necessary. In the survey, companies with top-quintile decision scores outperformed other companies by about 15 to 20 percent *in every single organizational area.* Moreover, the more elements of organizational health a company scored highly on, the higher its overall decision effectiveness. In short, an organization is a system, and all the elements have to work together to produce great results.

Benchmarking the organization

Using this kind of survey, a company can compile an organization scorecard much like the decision scorecard. Executives can find out which ailments the organization is suffering from. But this time, executives are looking at root causes, not just symptoms. The decision scorecard may indicate poor performance on, say, decision speed. The organization scorecard will reveal the reasons.

Hospira conducted an extensive organizational survey along with its investigation into decision effectiveness. The scorecard based on this survey showed significant strengths. The company had good leadership, for instance, and a strong talent pipeline. But it definitely showed symptoms of two ailments: decision ambiguity and process paralysis. People felt that decisions weren't always made at the right level of the organization and that the balance between the corporate center and the operating units wasn't on the mark. They believed that the decision processes were flawed: meetings weren't used well, interactions around decisions weren't mapped clearly, and so on. Also, the culture needed attention. Not everybody in the organization acted like an owner and made decisions reflecting the company's best interests. Not everyone brought a customer focus to decisions.

Thanks to these diagnoses, Hospira was able to redesign a wide variety of key decisions, and it began reshaping the organization to support and enable continued good decision making and execution. These efforts involved extensive training as well as strong leadership engagement on the organizational changes that would help take Hospira from good to great. As we write, the company has come far on its journey. One early win was those marketing brochures. A team redesigned the process required to design and approve a set of marketing materials, reducing approval time substantially. (You'll read more about this in chapter 4.) Hospira has been making similar gains in many other decision areas. If it can consistently improve on decision speed and effort while maintaining quality and yield, it should achieve its ambitious plans. Already, the company has achieved results well ahead of its 2009 cost and revenue targets. And the stock price was up more than 80 percent since the announcement of the transformation efforts, with total shareholder returns in the upper quartile—right where Begley and his team believed they should have been.

A quick test of your organization's effectiveness

Now let's begin to take stock of your own organization's decision effectiveness, along with the organizational strengths and weaknesses that affect it.

What you'll find here, of course, isn't our full survey. The complete survey is a comprehensive assessment that explores every element of an organization, from the clarity of accountabilities for making and executing decisions to the behaviors exhibited by its leadership. We typically survey a broad sample from multiple areas and levels of the business, and we generate rich sets of data. Benchmarks on each organizational dimension help companies identify the most debilitating ailments and highlight opportunities to improve performance.

But you can get things started with the set of simplified assessment tools presented here. This "*Cosmo* quiz" approach won't show you all of the decision breakdowns that may be ailing your company, and it won't provide the basis for a detailed plan to improve decision effectiveness. But it will accomplish three important objectives. It will help you establish a preliminary benchmark for how your organization stacks up on decision effectiveness relative to our sample of more than 750 companies. It will shed light on the broad strengths and weaknesses of your organization in getting things decided and delivered. And it will give you an indication of whether a deeper investigation and assessment are warranted.

The decision scorecard

Begin by taking the quick test about decisions shown in figure 2-1. There is one question on each of the four elements of decision effectiveness—quality, speed, yield, and effort. Thinking about the most important strategic and operational decisions you have been involved in at your company over the last three years, circle 1, 2, 3, or 4 for each question as it relates to those critical decisions.

Now tally your overall score like this. First, multiply your scores for quality (Q), speed (S), and yield (Y) to get your QSY product. If your scores are 3, 4, and 2, for example, your QSY product is 24. Next, divide your effort (E) score by 4, and multiply the result by the QSY product. If you're putting in exactly the right amount of effort, your tax is zero and you're multiplying by 1, so your QSY product doesn't change. But if you scored effort as a 25 percent tax, then your after-tax score is 3/4, or 75 percent, of the QSY product. In this example, your score would be 18. (Note that we have simplified the calculations to make the quiz easier; dividing this effort score by 4 is equivalent to subtracting effort in our standard formula.)

Using our database, you can now compare your decision score with the performance ranges for each benchmark quartile. If you score over 25, you are performing at the level of the top-quartile companies in our survey. Relative to our sample, your organization appears to decide and deliver.

The organization scorecard

Now take the quick test for organizational health shown in figure 2-2. In lieu of our full survey, we have included ten high-level

FIGURE 2-1

Decision scorecard "quick test"

Quality (Q)	When making critical decisions, we choose the right course of action: 4 - >75% of the time 3 - 51–75% of the time 2 - 26–50% of the time 1 - ≤25% of the time	1	2	3	4
Speed (S)	We make critical decisions: 4 - Much faster than competitors 3 - Somewhat faster than competitors 2 - Somewhat slower than competitors 1 - Much slower than competitors	1	2	3	4
Yield (Y)	We execute critical decisions as intended: 4 - >75% of the time 3 - 51–75% of the time 2 - 26–50% of the time 1 - ≤25% of the time	1	2	3	4
Effort (E)	In making and executing critical decisions: 4 - We put in exactly the right amount of effort 3 - We put in somewhat too much/too little effort versus the amount we should 2 - We put in way too much/nowhere near enough effort versus the amount we should 1 - We're off the charts	1	2	3	4

Instructions

- Read each question and circle the score that corresponds to the answer that best fits your organization
- To get your total score, multiply the first 3 scores together. Then multiply that result by the Effort score divided by 4
- For example, if you circle 3, 4, 2, 3, you would calculate your total as 3 x 4 x 2 x [3/4]=18

Total Score
$[Q \times S \times Y \times (E/4)]$
Note: In this quiz, multiplying the product of Q, S, Y by the score for E/4 is a shortcut to get to (QSY-E) in our standard formula.

>25 = Top quartile—You're doing great, keep it up
21–25 = Second quartile—Pretty good, but could be great
16–20 = Third quartile—Worse than 50% of companies, time to act!
15 or less = Bottom quartile—Major decision reboot required!

FIGURE 2-2

Organization scorecard "quick test"

		Strongly disagree	Disagree more than agree	Agree more than disagree	Strongly agree
Structure	Our structure helps, rather than hinders, the decisions most critical to our success.	1	2	3	4
Roles	Individuals are clear on their roles and accountabilities in our most critical decisions.	1	2	3	4
Processes	Our processes are designed to produce effective, timely decisions and action.	1	2	3	4
Information	The people in critical decision roles have the information they need when and how they need it.	1	2	3	4
Measures and incentives	Our measures and incentives focus people on making and executing effective decisions.	1	2	3	4
Priorities	People understand their priorities clearly enough to be able to make and execute the decisions they face.	1	2	3	4
Decision style	We make decisions in a style that is effective; for example, a style that appropriately balances inclusiveness with momentum.	1	2	3	4
People	We put our best people in the jobs where they can have the biggest decision impact.	1	2	3	4
Behaviors	Our leaders at all levels consistently demonstrate effective decision behaviors.	1	2	3	4
Culture	Our culture reinforces prompt, effective decisions and action throughout the organization.	1	2	3	4

Total score (Add all scores) _____ (Min = 10, Max = 40)

>35 = Top quartile—You're doing great, keep it up
31–35 = Second quartile—Good but room for improvement
26–30 = Third quartile—Org is serious barrier to decisions
10–25 = Fourth quartile—Major org transformation required

Instructions

- Read each question and circle the score that matches your level of agreement/disagreement with the statement
- 1 = Strongly disagree, 2 = Disagree more than agree, 3 = Agree more than disagree, 4 = Strongly agree
- To get your total score, add up your individual scores

statements that approximate the content of each part of the longer survey. (Remember, these are the issues most highly correlated with decision effectiveness.) Each of the ten organizational ailments we described earlier links to the statements here.

To get a total, simply score each statement 1 to 4, and then add up your scores. Here, too, you can compare your total score with the performance of companies in our database. A score above 35 puts you in the top quartile—your organization is pretty healthy. A score of 31 to 35 indicates room for improvement but no immediate signs of organizational breakdowns. A score of 30 or below, by contrast, indicates that you definitely have some organizational challenges to address. If you perform at less than a 2.5 on any one issue, it's likely that this particular ailment needs treatment. Of course, if your score is quite low, you will undoubtedly want to do more research—with a broader sample, richer benchmarks, more questions, and so forth.

Filling in these two quick surveys allows you to summarize your performance, as in figures 2-3 and 2-4. (The two figures

FIGURE 2-3

Decision scorecard "readout" example

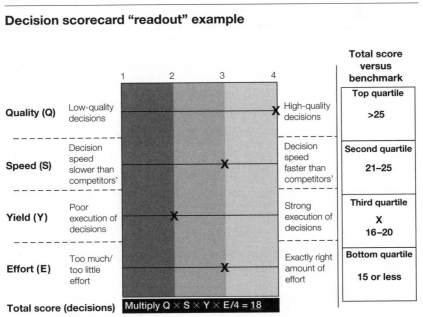

FIGURE 2-4

Organization score card "readout" example

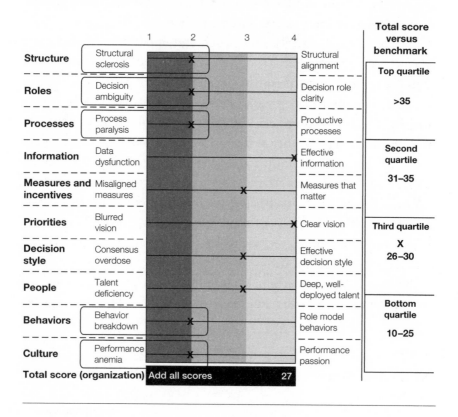

The figure shows a score card table with decision elements scored on a scale of 1 to 4, and a "Total score versus benchmark" column:

	Negative condition	1	2	3	4	Positive condition	Total score versus benchmark
Structure	Structural sclerosis		X			Structural alignment	**Top quartile** >35
Roles	Decision ambiguity		X			Decision role clarity	
Processes	Process paralysis		X			Productive processes	
Information	Data dysfunction				X	Effective information	**Second quartile** 31–35
Measures and incentives	Misaligned measures			X		Measures that matter	
Priorities	Blurred vision				X	Clear vision	**Third quartile** X 26–30
Decision style	Consensus overdose			X		Effective decision style	
People	Talent deficiency			X		Deep, well-deployed talent	
Behaviors	Behavior breakdown		X			Role model behaviors	**Bottom quartile** 10–25
Culture	Performance anemia		X			Performance passion	
Total score (organization)	Add all scores				27		

show the scores of an anonymous company drawn from our database.)

The company in this example shows good performance on decision quality but lower results on all the other decision elements, especially yield (figure 2-3). Its overall decision score is thus $(4 \times 3 \times 2) \times (3/4) = 18$. That's a third-quartile score, so it's definitely time to act. The company's overall organization score is 27 out of a possible 40—also the third quartile—with five ailments (circled) that require attention (figure 2-4). The assessment indicates a clear case for change and gives a broad indication of which issues need to be tackled.

This quick survey will at least give you an idea of how Hospira and other companies have assessed their decision effectiveness and organizational health. Companies that have done the complete assessment know where their greatest decision challenges lie and what organizational ailments they are suffering from. Their management teams are typically aligned around the need to change and have seen how they can best tackle the opportunities.

Then comes the next step: identifying the company's critical decisions. After all, you can't design an organization around decisions without knowing which decisions to focus on.

[3]

Focus on the Decisions
That Matter Most

It had been an interesting weekend. Alan Mulally, then CEO of Boeing's Commercial Airplanes division, had spent it with Bill Ford and Ford's family outside Detroit. Mulally mostly listened. Ford told how his family's once-great auto company had come to the brink of collapse. He proposed that Mulally replace him as CEO. Mulally hadn't ever thought of working anywhere but Boeing—after all, he had been there since 1969, and it was now 2006. But Ford Motor Company really needed help. And Mulally began to think that he might be able to offer some.

Not much later, Mulally arrived at Ford's headquarters to begin his new job. Things were every bit as bad as Bill Ford had described. The company's finances were shaky, and its future uncertain. Ford had lost about a point of market share every year for the past ten years. Mulally himself wasn't exactly welcomed with open arms. Only a "car guy," the traditionalists felt, could turn Ford around—and Mulally was hardly that. He had never set foot in a Detroit assembly plant. He even drove a Japanese car.

But Mulally had a different approach. Like everybody else, he could see that Ford had too many unrelated brands, too little commonality across its car models, too many financially troubled suppliers and dealers, and too much reliance on big SUVs and trucks. Indeed, the company had decades of internal analyses and consulting studies documenting these difficulties. But Mulally also saw that no one at Ford was addressing those issues. People were stuck in a rut. They weren't making and executing the important decisions. They had to start doing so now—before time ran out.

YOUR OWN ORGANIZATION may not be in quite such dire straits as Ford was in 2006—at least we hope it isn't. But when you assess decision making and execution, you're likely to find both big challenges and big opportunities. You may find, as many leaders do, that decision making and execution need a step-change improvement. You may find that your organization is suffering from two or three ailments. If that's the case, then you have an opportunity to register big performance gains by fixing the problems—by building an organization that can truly decide and deliver. The rest of this book will help you achieve that goal.

So let's continue on our five-step process. Step two is to identify your most important decisions, those that will have the greatest impact on results when you get them right.

Knowing your organization's most important decisions is like finding a key that opens a lot of different locks. It allows you to concentrate your efforts on what's essential. It helps people who work in different units or functions cut through the complexity they face every day. It helps them understand with whom they should collaborate and why. If you get the most important decisions working right, moreover, you'll see a spillover effect to other decisions. Your organization's "decision muscles" will get stronger.

And if you fail to identify the most important decisions, what happens then? The symptoms are all too familiar. The executive team spends an hour debating the organization's laptop policy instead of fundamental strategy issues. The senior brand team argues too long about which color to use on a new brochure and not long enough about when and how to launch a new product. Often, the misdirection of attention is subtle and becomes obvious only in retrospect. The senior executive committee of a large European bank spent a lot of time before the 2008 financial meltdown discussing decisions related to the bank's income statement. It spent hardly any time on decisions related to the balance sheet, yet it was balance-sheet risk that eventually undermined the bank's stability. Without an accurate sense of which decisions matter most, an organization can end up making the important ones on the fly, without the attention they deserve—or, often worse, delaying them again and again.

Our experience with clients over the years reveals stark differences relating to critical decisions. When companies truly understand which decisions matter most—and not just at the top but throughout the company—their organizations consistently do better on decision making and execution. Research bears out this observation. In our survey, organizations that were clear on their critical decisions scored an average 40 percent higher than others on decision effectiveness. Top-quintile companies on decision effectiveness were more than twice as likely to understand which decisions were most important. And this pattern extended beyond senior leaders. Frontline managers of top-quintile companies were almost three times as likely as others to say they knew what their critical decisions were.

A focus on critical decisions may have been the single most important change that Mulally brought to Ford. As he himself told us, "I think the Ford story is about making the decisions that needed to be made and then getting them to stick."

Beginning his first week at Ford, Mulally instituted a weekly meeting of the executive team. Called the Business Plan Review meeting, or BPR, it was a half-day session held at Ford's Dearborn headquarters. The first few BPRs were rough. Ford's senior leadership team couldn't agree on the company's problems, let alone its priorities. But Mulally kept at it. He pushed people to identify the most important decisions in their areas. He hammered on the idea that Ford had to confront its challenges now. Soon the meetings began to work. In just four short weeks, the team dissected the company's operations—everything from Ford's approach to new technology and the stability of the company's supply base to the strength of its brands and the performance of its dealers. Mulally summarized Ford's critical decisions for the company's board, spelling out on just one page the essentials for fixing Ford's business, including improvements to the quality and fuel efficiency of the company's cars, a reduction in the number of suppliers, rationalization of the dealer network, international expansion, and a strengthening of the balance sheet. While most of these critical decisions were not new, the crisp identification of the most important items helped everyone at Ford concentrate on what had to be done.

So the team debated the decisions and then began to make and execute them. Over a period of months, Ford reorganized its operations, moving from a regional business unit structure to a global matrix. It divested the Aston Martin, Jaguar, Land Rover, and (later) Volvo brands. It accelerated the development of new models, thereby strengthening its position in small, fuel-efficient cars. It took steps to reduce the number of vehicle platforms from more than forty to fewer than ten worldwide. It increased the proportion of common parts from less than 10 percent to more than 50 percent. And it cut the number of options configurations, reducing manufacturing complexity and improving the odds of getting the right vehicles on the dealers' lots. Mulally and his team also refinanced the company (raising more than $23 billion in secured financing), reached a breakthrough agreement with the United Auto Workers union, and began consolidating both suppliers and dealers. As this book went to press, Ford Motor Company still faced many challenges, and its future was far from certain. We have no crystal ball. Still, the company had already returned to solvency without the help of a bailout from the American taxpayer. It was gaining market share, and employee morale was higher than it had been in decades. If Ford could keep up the pace of making and executing its critical decisions, the automaker seemed likely to return to profitability by 2011, as Mulally was forecasting.

However the Ford saga turns out, it holds a powerful lesson. Like Ford, your organization can identify its critical decisions. Doing so will enable you to make and execute them better than before and will ensure that your efforts to improve decision effectiveness have a real impact on performance. In this chapter, we'll outline a structured approach to help you determine what those decisions are. We'll also describe a tool we call the *decision X-ray*, which will expose the trouble spots and help you figure out how to eliminate them.

Two categories of critical decisions

An organization's critical decisions typically fall into two broad categories.

Category one includes big decisions that carry enormous value. Many of these relate directly to the organization's strategy. When PETsMART decided to move into pet services, when Starbucks introduced its instant coffee, when Barclays decided to buy Lehman Brothers' U.S. assets—all these were important strategic decisions. This category also includes significant, onetime operational decisions, such as Applied Materials' decision to move its manufacturing and engineering base to Asia, and big, infrequent organizational decisions, such as a major restructuring. Finally, the category includes major financial decisions, such as Ford's choice not to take bailout funds from the U.S. government and not to file for bankruptcy protection. These decisions have to be made and executed effectively to create (and avoid destroying) shareholder value. Accordingly, any individual decision that has a large amount of value at stake is likely to count as critical.

The second category of critical decisions includes those that are made and remade frequently and that add up to a substantial amount of value over time. For instance, Amazon.com's continuing success can be attributed partly to a host of savvy merchandising decisions, including decisions about special prices and shipping discounts, suggestions for complementary purchases, and targeted e-mail notices about new offerings. Many of these decisions are made and remade every day, and none by itself carries much value. Together, however, they stimulate many millions of dollars in sales and contribute to a winning customer experience. Even seemingly mundane decisions such as how frontline clerks decide to treat customers can make a big difference over time. Timpson, the highly successful chain of key cutters and shoe repairers in the United Kingdom, is known for giving its customer-service staff broad latitude to make refund decisions up to a certain threshold, on the assumption that these employees have the information needed to make the best decisions. The policy helps generate a high level of customer satisfaction, one factor contributing to Timpson's strong performance: between 1996 and 2006, the company's revenues tripled and profit increased fivefold. Employee satisfaction has also been a winner. Timpson was consistently in the top ten of the *Sunday Times*'s original "100 Best Companies to Work For" list.

As this second category suggests, critical decisions are not the exclusive purview of senior executives and the board. On the contrary, every part of an enterprise has critical decisions of its own. IT departments, for instance, must make major decisions about systems investments. They also make routine but often essential decisions about matters such as software upgrades and help-desk staffing levels. Every business unit, function, and team may find it useful to develop its own list of critical decisions, so that it is always focusing on what's most important. If you're the leader of one of these units, you can see whether the critical decisions are being made well and quickly and whether they are executed as intended. You can also begin to see where strengthening the organization might be necessary to improve decision effectiveness.

Identifying your critical decisions

Here's a simple two-step process that will help you identify your own critical decisions.

Create a decision architecture

A decision architecture lays out a list of decisions for every major business process of a given company or unit. It shows the value-creation steps that the business or unit is responsible for. It identifies the key decisions, both one-off and ongoing, in each one. Depending upon the business, a decision architecture may contain dozens of decisions. Done right, it gives you a holistic view, enabling you to home in on the decisions that are central to success. It ensures that you have thought through all the possibilities and that you don't miss any important decisions.

Winnow the list

The next step is to shorten the list of decisions to those you most need to focus on. Companies typically employ two distinct screens as they narrow down their lists.

Screen number one is *value at stake*. Critical decisions, by definition, carry a high value. Knowing your company's strategy, you can determine which decisions will be most important to delivering value in the coming few years. To make sure you don't miss the everyday decisions that add up over time, you can keep in mind a handy formula: *value multiplied by frequency*. A national wireless phone operator, for instance, had decided on a strategy of growth outside its home market, where the company already held a substantial market share. So every decision about major international acquisitions would be key to implementing the strategy. The European rental-car company that we mentioned in chapter 2 realized that its growth would come from serving high-value international travelers, which it had failed to serve well in the past. So it put a high priority on everyday operating decisions about pricing, customer service, and fleet management—everything necessary to provide these travelers with a seamless experience. We don't propose you try to put a precise value on every decision; a rough idea of relative value is typically sufficient.

Screen number two is the *degree of management attention required*. Some decisions need more management attention than others if they are to work well. Why so? There are several possible reasons:

- *Complexity.* Decisions involving many stakeholders or complex processes with multiple handoffs may require a lot of attention and effort to get right.

- *Degree of change.* If a decision is likely to be affected by a proposed change, such as a new organizational structure, those involved will need to know how it is supposed to work in the future.

- *Scope for improvement.* A decision that's not working probably needs more attention than one that's going well.

- *Utility as a pilot.* Some decisions (or sets of decisions) may be particularly useful as pilots for improving decision effectiveness. At Hospira, many people knew that the marketing brochures were a problem. Fixing the process showed the benefits of the new decision-effectiveness effort.

The output from these two screens is a list of *critical decisions*. These are the top twenty or thirty, or whatever it may be— the most important decisions for a given company or area of the business. These decisions must work well if the organization is to better its performance.

At Ford, for example, the rallying cry for fixing the company's operations and generating what Mulally refers to as "profitable growth for all" was a simple schematic depicting the company's decision architecture (figure 3-1). The diagram outlined Ford's value chain—everything from the development of new automotive technologies to products, consumer credit, and after-sales service. Each step in the chain was roughly proportional to Ford's participation in that stage relative to what Mulally believed was optimal. In the case of suppliers, brands, and dealers, for example, Ford needed to narrow its participation. By contrast, Ford needed to broaden its geographic footprint, its investment in advanced technology, and its market share. Most important, the diagram spelled out the critical decisions that needed to be made

FIGURE 3-1

Ford's decision architecture and critical decisions

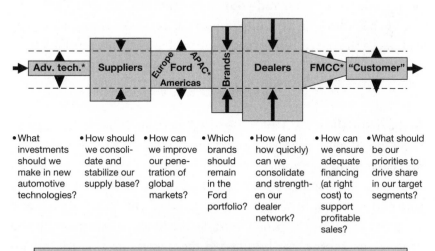

| • What investments should we make in new automotive technologies? | • How should we consolidate and stabilize our supply base? | • How can we improve our penetration of global markets? | • Which brands should remain in the Ford portfolio? | • How (and how quickly) can we consolidate and strengthen our dealer network? | • How can we ensure adequate financing (at right cost) to support profitable sales? | • What should be our priorities to drive share in our target segments? |

Infrastructure/team

- • How can we work together more effectively as a team?
- • What investment should we make in global infrastructure?
- • What actions should we take to strengthen our balance sheet?

*Adv. tech. = advanced technologies; APAC = Asia-Pacific; FMCC = Ford Motor Credit Company at each step, as well as the supporting infrastructure that would be required. Every week, Mulally and his team tracked their progress in making and executing these decisions. Their relentless focus on the critical decisions enabled people to move quickly and in concert to restore profitability.

In practice, companies tailor this two-step process to their own situation. Some take a comprehensive approach, listing decision areas (such as brand management) and then identifying important decisions within each area (such as the target customer segment for each brand). Once they have a long list of decisions, they use surveys, interviews, and workshops to assess the value and degree of attention required and thus winnow down the list. Other companies, such as Ford, take a simpler, more intuitive approach. They create a high-level architecture with decision areas, assign priorities to each area, and brainstorm critical decisions only in the areas with the highest priority. Either approach can work, and both are likely to produce twenty to thirty decisions to focus on. Your own method will depend on the urgency of the situation, the clarity of your company's strategic priorities (which tell you what the important decisions are), and your organization's culture.

Let's see how some companies have applied the two-step critical decisions process, starting with British American Tobacco.

British American Tobacco

In the first half of the 1990s, British American Tobacco (BAT) was made up of four operating companies. Each had its own brands, and each had geographic areas where it was the dominant player. An operating company that sold one of its brands on another's turf had to do so through a licensing agreement. When Russia and Eastern Europe were opened to trade, the four companies competed against one another for business in these new markets. All, for instance, had separate representative offices in Moscow. The idea was that competition would spur better performance from each unit.

Martin Broughton, who took over the top job at BAT in 1993, thought this approach was wasteful and inefficient. He was tired of the joke, he said, that "there are seven major tobacco companies in the world—and four of them are British American Tobacco." He wanted everyone in BAT to think of external competitors such as Philip Morris—and not BAT's other divisions—as the enemy. He believed that pursuing one unified strategy—"one BAT"—would allow BAT to overtake Philip Morris as the leading tobacco company worldwide, a position it had lost years before. He estimated that synergies in global brand management, global sourcing, and other areas would allow the company to realize hundreds of millions of dollars a year in incremental profit.

Nor was it Broughton alone who felt the need for change. Employees throughout the business were frustrated. David Crow, then a regional marketing executive with the BATCO operating division, described a visit he paid to Brown & Williamson, the U.S.–based sister division. "I was the first BATCO person who had been there at an operational level—ever," he recalls. "It took us about three days just to get on with doing business." Adds David Fell, who was marketing director for Malaysia at the time: "When I first joined BATCO in 1989, I thought I had joined one company. But I quickly found out that I had joined four—if not five."

Broughton knew the key to his plan would be to get the organization to make and execute decisions in a radically different way. But which decisions needed the most attention? Much of BAT's success would still depend on great execution in local markets, which was already working well. But BAT needed major changes in other areas. Starting with an overall decision architecture for their industry, Broughton's team quickly homed in on four key decision areas that were critical to the company's transformation (figure 3-2).

- *Brand portfolio.* The company had a wide, diverse portfolio of brands, some of which competed directly with one another. Now the team would have to decide in a coordinated fashion which brands BAT would maintain and invest in.

- *Management of global brands.* Some of BAT's brands, such as Lucky Strike, were sold in many markets, and

FIGURE 3-2

British American Tobacco's decision architecture

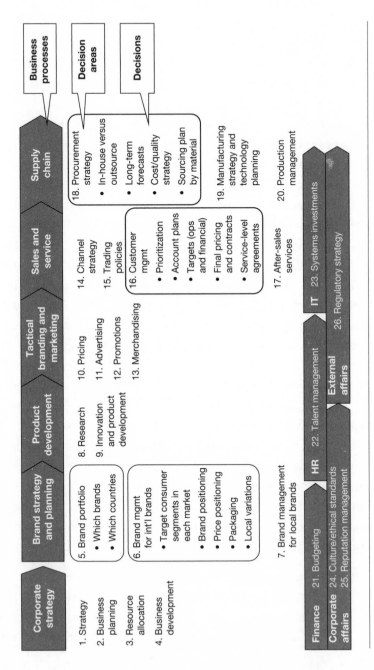

global brand recognition was essential to their success. So decisions about how to position, package, and price the brands couldn't be left solely to the discretion of local operations—a global role was required.

- *Procurement of selected commodities.* The company's procurement of commodities was fragmented. BAT now hoped to capitalize on its global scale by working with global suppliers wherever possible. Much tobacco still had to be supplied locally to satisfy local tastes. But commodities such as tow, a component of filters, could be sourced globally.

- *Customer management.* While the other decision areas benefited from an increased global role, the team wanted to keep much of customer management local. Most of the value in each country came from national accounts, where responsiveness was critical. New advertising restrictions in some markets made local customer relationships even more important. But the team also wanted to ensure the sharing of best practices among countries. The aim was to give local organizations as much firepower as possible for the "war in the store."

Good, timely, and well-executed decisions in these four areas would be essential to the success of the new strategy and would contribute significant value to the new company. Moreover, three of the four—all but customer management—were likely to undergo substantial change as the company moved to its new global model. They represented a new challenge for the organization, and Broughton was relying on decisions in those areas to generate much of the incremental value.

Once they had agreed on the most critical decisions in each of the four priority areas, team members could start on the more difficult process of making them work. They defined roles and accountabilities. They designed end-to-end decision processes. They modified the organization's structure to break down the boundaries and to bring the four separate operating companies into one business with a single board. For BAT, the effects of these changes were extraordinary. Under Broughton, the company increased its share of international brands, lowered its costs, and improved its operating margins. Its stock outperformed the FTSE International 100 by fivefold between 1988 and 2008, and its revenue grew faster than that of major competitors between 2000 and 2008.

MetLife

As BAT shows, key decisions don't just happen at the top. So companies have to identify important decisions wherever these occur in the business—at the center, in regions, in local markets—and ensure that all such decisions are working well. MetLife, a $50 billion global insurance giant headquartered in New York City, recognized this. Indeed, the company's ambitious leadership team saw that improving decision capabilities throughout the organization could be a powerful competitive weapon, fueling growth and accelerating delivery of operational excellence initiatives. MetLife's decision and organizational scorecards indicated that overall scores on decisions were good, but there were significant opportunities to improve on speed and effort. This pattern showed up in most areas of the business.

After working through the critical decisions at the enterprise level, executives led similar exercises at each business unit and corporate function. Teams developed their own lists of top decisions, coming up with twenty or so in each area that carried high value and had significant room for improvement. For instance, people in the Auto & Home division spent time in workshops thinking through their strategic priorities and the major decisions that needed to work well. Identifying twenty-four critical decisions, they assigned eight of these to the leaders of their executive team, asking the leaders to come back with recommendations on how to make the decisions work better. One example was setting priorities for discretionary IT projects. Long a sore point among executives, these decisions sucked up time and energy yet left people frustrated, because the choices didn't always support strategic goals. MetLife redefined this process and clarified the roles involved, thereby reducing the work and increasing the quality of the decisions. This and other early wins allowed Auto & Home to build momentum for improving decision effectiveness. Clarifying the important decisions enabled the teams to focus their efforts on areas that would most affect their bottom line.

Pipavav Shipyard Limited

Identifying critical decisions is vital to improving the performance of any established organization such as BAT or MetLife. It's equally important in a start-up, or when a company enters new market segments. An example is Pipavav Shipyard Limited, jointly launched by SKIL Infrastructure and the engineering company Punj Lloyd. When complete, Pipavav will be the largest shipyard in India. It is strategically located on India's west coast, on the route between Singapore and the Arabian Gulf. In 2009 the company began construction on an order for twenty-six vessels, which was worth more than $1 billion. It also has contracts for a number of other ship programs.

Pipavav's initial focus was on commercial tankers. But the company had ambitious plans to scale up quickly in several other market segments, such as naval ships and offshore equipment. To do that, its leaders knew, Pipavav would need efficient, effective decision making and execution. Through a series of interviews and discussions, the management team identified twenty-two decisions that would determine the success or failure of the growth plans. One set involved developing the right offer in each business—the range of services, pricing, lead times, and so forth. These decisions needed to be on target for the businesses to prosper. Another set of decisions related to the optimal use of the critical shared resource, dock space. Which contracts should Pipavav bid on when bidding involved trade-offs between business lines? Should one business agree to changes in order specs if the changes would affect ship programs in other businesses?

Identifying these decisions allowed the team to define who would play specific roles in each decision. Decision authority was left to the business unit heads for all the decisions that affected only one business line. Decisions would come to the CEO only when trade-offs and coordination were necessary across business lines. The focus on critical decisions allowed Pipavav to zero in on potential bottlenecks and get them out of the way before they hampered the company's growth.

Using a decision X-ray to analyze critical decisions

Once you have a clear sense of your organization's critical decisions and have highlighted the ones that most need improvement, it's always tempting to jump right in and fix things. But it's often more productive, we've found, to analyze selected decisions in greater depth first. How are they working right now? Where are the failings, exactly—quality, speed, yield, effort, or some combination of the four? What aspects of the organization are holding the decisions back?

To reach that level of specificity, we use a tool called a decision X-ray. Just as a physician wouldn't reset a broken arm without X-raying it first, leaders would have a tough time resetting decisions without a deeper picture of the challenges each one faces. In a decision X-ray, leaders ask questions of everyone involved in the selected decisions. How do they rate quality, speed, yield, and effort? Who plays what roles, and are the roles clear to all? How well does the process work? Where is the organization helping or hurting? What behaviors get in the way? A decision X-ray often uncovers issues that a broad survey misses. It can reveal the kinds of actions likely to improve problem areas. It also may turn up issues common to many key decisions.

Nike

Nike's Europe, Middle East, and Africa division is one organization that found decision X-rays helpful in highlighting specific problems and opportunities. Nike, of course, is one of the world's most successful sports companies and has for years been a leader in three businesses: sports-related footwear, apparel, and equipment. The company's organizational structure and processes had long been a matrix, with the three businesses on one dimension and geographic areas on the other. In 2007, however, executives began to believe that they were missing a holistic focus on a given sport *across* the three business areas, and so they introduced a sport-focused dimension to the matrix. With their "Just Do It" attitude, people at Nike mostly welcomed the change, realizing it would bring them closer to consumers. But they also knew they needed to get on top of the ambiguity the new structure would create. Otherwise, they might have trouble responding quickly to changing market trends across countries, products, and sports.

To uncover the issues that needed attention, Nike identified ten major decision areas: category selection, budgeting and targeting, channel/sales strategy, and so on. Then the company came up with thirty-three key decisions under the ten headings. Team members dissected the decisions to see what was really going on. They used surveys to get broad input on all thirty-three, and they conducted detailed X-ray-style interviews to get more insight into a few of these key decisions.

The X-rays highlighted a need to modify decision roles and processes. One set of decisions, for instance, involved how much to invest in new-product development. In the previous system, the business unit (such as apparel or footwear) would make the decision. But should the business unit continue to do so in the new system, with input from the category organization? Or should the roles be reversed? Survey respondents had a range of views both on how the decisions worked today and on how they should work in the future, with perhaps predictable differences on country versus center, and category versus sport. Decisions regarding retail strategy for each country showed similar differences.

Nike, of course, wasn't just interested in diagnosing the issues. The company used the decision X-rays to help resolve them. In workshops, managers clarified how specific decisions should be made in the new matrix. They also proposed other practical changes, such as co-locating project teams that had previously been dispersed throughout the building. That made it easier for teams to communicate and collaborate, and for Nike to deploy teams quickly to the hottest opportunities, whether it was basketball in Poland or swimwear in Germany. The one-two punch of identifying its critical decisions and then X-raying them to determine specific fixes helped Nike get the new matrix working without missing a beat in performance.

How to conduct a decision X-ray

Conducting a set of decision X-rays is a good way to push ahead on improving decision effectiveness. You'll no doubt want to pick some decisions that are not working well today. You may find it equally instructive to contrast those with one or two that do work well.

The overall goal is to assess the effectiveness of the particular decision and what's holding it back. There are several ways to go about it. You can gather people in a room (physical or virtual), conduct a series of interviews, or send out a broader online survey. Start with gauging quality, speed, yield, and effort. Then assess which organizational elements may be standing in the way of an effective decision (figure 3-3). Questions about each of the organizational ailments we introduced in chapter 2 can serve as a helpful checklist. Of course, if an area is particularly strong, you'll want to note that, too. Decision effectiveness is as much about building on strengths as it is about fixing weaknesses.

As part of the X-ray, it's often helpful to sketch out a "day in the life of a decision" (figure 3-4). This shows what a decision has to go through—the loops, disconnects, and misalignments that slow things down and push people toward lowest-common-denominator solutions. Mapping the *actual* steps a decision goes through, rather than the ideal steps encapsulated in a process guide, for example, often leads to a "How could we have let that happen?" moment. It inspires people to consider significant changes. It also provides concrete ideas on how to fix the problem. Looking

FIGURE 3-3

Decision X-ray "snapshot"

Decision: [write decision here]

Decision effective-ness	Quality In retrospect, we made the right decision:	Speed Relative to competitors, we made the decision:	Yield We executed the decision as intended:	Effort The level of effort we applied was:
	4 – Strongly agree 3 – Agree 2 – Disagree 1 – Strongly disagree	4 – Much faster 3 – Somewhat faster 2 – Somewhat slower 1 – Much slower	4 – Strongly agree 3 – Agree 2 – Disagree 1 – Strongly disagree	4 – Exactly the right amount 3 – A bit too much/little 2 – Way too much/too little 1 – Off the charts

Organization strengths/barriers	Rating 4 – Strongly agree; 3 – Agree; 2 – Disagree; 1 – Strongly disagree	Comments
• Our structure facilitated making and executing the decision well and quickly with the right effort		
• Decision roles were clear and appropriate		
• We used a robust decision process		
• We had the right information at the right time		
• People's objectives and incentives reinforced the right decision and action		
• Participants had the right context to make and execute the decision		
• We used an appropriate decision style		
• We had the right skills and talent in right decision roles		
• Participants demonstrated good decision behaviors		
• Our culture reinforced making and executing the decision well		

FIGURE 3-4

Decision X-ray "day in the life"

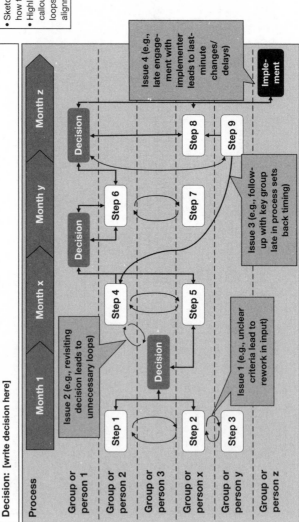

Decision: [write decision here]

| Process | Month 1 | Month x | Month y | Month z |

Group or person 1
Group or person 2
Group or person 3
Group or person x
Group or person y
Group or person z

Step 1
Step 2
Step 3
Step 4
Step 5
Step 6
Step 7
Step 8
Step 9

Decision
Decision
Decision
Decision

Implement

Issue 1 (e.g., unclear criteria lead to rework in input)

Issue 2 (e.g., revisiting decision leads to unnecessary loops)

Issue 3 (e.g., follow-up with key group late in process sets back timing)

Issue 4 (e.g., late engagement with implementer leads to last-minute changes/delays)

Instructions

- Sketch out the basic process steps for how the decision works today
- Highlight issues and disconnects in callouts, reflecting on unnecessary loops, process disconnects, and alignment issues

at organizational obstacles through the day-in-the-life lens can help you see what elements need to change.

Without a focus on critical decisions, attempts to reshape organizations inevitably have a kind of scattershot quality—a little bit here, a little bit there—and the teams leading the charge never really know whether the changes they're working so hard on will have a real effect. One of our clients referred to the phenomenon of "creeping egalitarianism," with every issue treated as equally important and none getting the attention it deserved. But once you view the organization with critical decisions in mind, you'll never look at it like that again. You'll know that *those* are the decisions that must work smoothly. You'll know that improving effectiveness on the critical decisions will lead to higher performance.

Now let's see how organizations can make their critical decisions work better.

[4]

Make Individual Decisions Work

Tim Beckman, the chief operating officer of International Energy, slammed down the phone. * *He was furious.*

A few weeks before, he had finally decided to scrap his company's T662 turbine, a product that just wasn't selling. The decision hadn't been easy. In fact, his first call was to overrule his subordinates and keep the T662 on the market. But after a while, he had to admit that the others were right. The product was a bust and should be killed.

And now? Now he had just learned that the factory in California had completely ignored his latest decision and continued to crank out T662s. Even worse, nobody had bothered to cancel the plant's big supply contracts, which extended eighteen months. So the company faced huge liabilities to suppliers if it stuck to its guns and canceled the product. That changed the economics of the situation, and he would have to reevaluate the decision once more.

---

*The executive's name, the company's name, and the specific industry in this story have been changed.

He cursed. This was truly the product that wouldn't die. Or maybe it should be called the decision that wouldn't stick. How did things ever reach this point?

LIKE THE COMPANY we're calling International Energy, too many companies fail to make and execute their critical decisions well. Some organizations simply dither. Others make a decision, then revisit it repeatedly. Still others make poor choices or are unable to translate their decisions into action. For decisions with a great deal of value at stake, the cost of all these failings can be extraordinarily high.

So the third step in our five-step process is to focus on selected critical decisions, those that give you the most trouble or are likely to do so in the future, and to make sure you're setting them up to be made and executed successfully. Just as you X-rayed them to learn what was going wrong, you can *reset* these decisions to get them humming the way they should. A decision reset, as we call this companion to the decision X-ray, is one of the most powerful tools you have at your disposal. It gets individual decisions working better. It also shows people that they can cut through bureaucratic logjams and get things decided and delivered. A reset is not unduly complex. It involves coming up with good answers to just four questions (figure 4-1):

- *What* decision needs to be made and executed?

- *Who* will play the key roles that go into a decision—not just making and implementing the decision but coming up with a recommendation or offering input?

- *How* will the decision be made and executed?

- *When* must the decision be made and executed to deliver the best possible performance?

FIGURE 4-1

Clarifying the "what-who-how-when" to make critical decisions hum

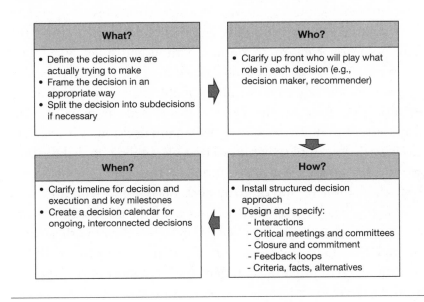

International Energy badly needed a reset—it stumbled on every one of these four questions. What follows is the whole sad story.

International Energy (IE) was the world's largest manufacturer of power turbines. In 1997, it acquired a major competitor, the number three player in the industry. The competitor—call it World Power—had its own line of turbines, including the new T662 model. IE adopted the T662 as its own, gave it a new name, and introduced it to the marketplace. Unfortunately, customers yawned. After nearly two years of lackluster sales, IE's head of Power Turbines decided to cancel the product.

But Tim Beckman, the CEO of World Power, had become chief operating officer (COO) of the newly merged IE, and he wasn't going to let his old company's latest and greatest product go to an early grave. He quickly countermanded the cancellation and asked for more data, saying he would make a final decision later. Three times, the Power Turbines staff came back with more data; three times, the COO let the T662 proceed. The next time, however, Beckman acquiesced and terminated the product.

Now we get to the source of Beckman's fury. The manager of the plant making the T662s was a former World Power supervisor who regarded the T662 as his baby. He had known about the fight going on back at corporate, a thousand miles away, and when the COO's latest decision came down, the manager decided to ignore it. Headquarters would probably change its mind again, he thought—after all, the T662 had survived the previous four decisions. His failure to execute Beckman's decision as instructed, along with the supplier liabilities that were piling up, led to three *more* reevaluations and three more decisions to kill the T662. Each time, though, the company postponed implementation.

Finally, headquarters decided to cancel the product, once and for all, and absorb the supplier liability. But then another party entered the discussion—IE's financing unit, known as IECC. IECC pointed out that the company had sold most of the T662s it produced to its own leasing company (a division of IECC), which leased them to customers. If IE discontinued the model, customers would be unlikely to renew their leases and the company would be left holding the bag. So now the decision had to be revisited once more. Again the turbine survived.

Ten times, the T662 supposedly died; ten times, it lived on. Not until the eleventh decision, more than four years after the first one, did IE finally put the last nail in the T662's coffin and halt production. Factoring in all the costs—the remaining supplier liabilities, the drop in value of the turbines that IE's leasing division owned, and so on—the company lost an estimated $2.5 billion on the product.

Examine this decision along the four dimensions we described—what, who, how, and when—and right away, you see why it was so badly fouled up.

First, people weren't sure for a while what decision they were making. The T662 decision was initially wrapped up in a broad discussion of "product line strategy." Not until well down the road did the team frame the issue specifically: "What should we do with the T662 to generate the most profit for the business?" Second, decision roles were about as murky as they could be. Was the head of Power Turbines responsible for the decision? Or was it the COO, the vice president of manufacturing, or somebody else entirely? Who knew? Then, too, who was to be held accountable for execution? (Apparently not the plant manager.)

Third, there was no well-defined process for making and executing the decision, which is why it had to be reevaluated so many times. No one laid out the facts from the outset, no one formulated alternatives or established criteria for evaluating them, and no one connected the decision to the allocation of resources. Since IE had no formal process to track whether the decision had been executed, the renegade plant manager could do his own thing and stay under the radar, at least for a while. Fourth, the company set no timetable or deadline for making and executing the decision. Had there been one, the process might not have dragged on so long.

So let's take a look at these four elements, the what, who, how, and when. Resets that bring you closer to best practice on each of them for your most important decisions will put you well along on the path to greater decision effectiveness.

Define the *what*

People need to know what decision they're making. That seems obvious, doesn't it? But most executives at one time or another have found themselves sitting in meetings wondering what decision the group was trying to make. That's because many companies repeatedly fail to define the *what* of critical decisions.

Clarity

The first and most obvious point is that people need to state the decision clearly. What exactly is the group trying to decide? "Today we're here to talk about XYZ" is a common meeting opener—and it says exactly nothing from a decision point of view. Are there any decisions on the agenda? If so, what are they? For a company to improve decision effectiveness, the decision at hand must be unambiguous to everyone.

Framing

Sometimes, the way you ask a question affects how it's answered. As J. Edward Russo and Paul J. H. Schoemaker explain in *Winning Decisions*, "the way people frame a problem—i.e., the particular perspective that they (often unconsciously) adopt—exerts enormous power over the options they will recognize and the solutions they will favor." The best companies frame decisions in ways that maximize the likelihood of a good outcome. For example, they avoid yes/no decisions such as "Should we pursue this strategy or not?" and instead opt for frames that get the creative juices flowing and produce better alternatives. When the team at Ford Motor Company was deciding whether to accept a bailout from U.S. taxpayers, for instance, Alan Mulally framed the decision as "What strategy will maximize the long-term value of the company?" This forced the group to examine alternatives such as "fix the operations," "merge with a competitor," "seek Chapter 11 bankruptcy protection," and others, along with accepting government funding. Only by framing the decision in this way—and not "Should we accept a bailout or not?"—was Ford able to make the best decision for all the company's stakeholders.

Unbundling

Even if a decision is clear and framed effectively, it may not in fact be a single decision; it may include several discrete decisions bundled together. Unbundling a decision into its component parts often helps a company speed things up. Think once more of the European division of an American automaker we worked with (see chapter 1). It found itself endlessly debating what seemed like a specific, well-framed decision, namely, which features were to be standard on a given model of a car. The reason for the wrangling was that both product development and marketing felt they should play the lead role. To cut through the logjam, the company learned to break this decision into two parts. The first established a menu of options that fit the cost guidelines. Product development took the lead here. The second selected features from that list, with a view of customer needs and the competition in mind. Marketing was responsible for that one. Unbundling the decision eliminated a lot of needless debate.

Tips for success

High-performing organizations have developed many techniques for ensuring that nobody is confused about what decision they are trying to make. Some of these tools are surprisingly simple:

- *Start any discussion on decisions with a reminder of what you're trying to decide.* Intel asks its employees to begin every meeting with a single statement: "The purpose of this meeting is to inform you about X, to discuss Y, and to decide on Z," where Z is a specific, well-defined decision. Not much ambiguity there. Another company we worked with takes this discipline one step further, reviewing decisions made in previous discussions that form the foundation for those being made in later conversations. Such disciplines force team leaders to specify the what of decisions.

- *Frame the decision in the reverse.* Reversing the framing often allows you to reexamine assumptions. Jim Collins, in *How the Mighty Fall*, examines the space shuttle *Challenger* disaster; he notes that the crucial go/no-go decision was framed as "Can you prove it's *unsafe* to launch?" instead of the more prudent "Can you prove it's *safe* to launch?" Reversing the framing, or at least asking both questions, might have averted the explosion that destroyed the space shuttle and killed the astronauts on board.

- *Make each decision explicit—and check to see if you are missing any parts of the decision.* Consider MetLife Auto & Home's decision on prioritizing projects for discretionary IT funds, discussed in chapter 3. In the past, people had proposed as many as one hundred projects, often with little regard to the division's strategic priorities. Each project had an equal claim on IT resources just to develop the proposal. Reviewing this situation, Auto & Home executives realized that there really should be two decisions, one of which was missing. First, they should decide what kinds of projects would support the division's current strategic priorities and thus merit a full proposal. Then they could decide which proposals to approve. Making that missing decision explicit led to far fewer proposals and a much more efficient use of time and money.

So the first task in analyzing any given decision is to ask yourself these questions. Do the relevant people know what decision they are trying to make? Is the decision properly framed so that the right choices are considered and discussed? Is it just one decision, or are there several decisions that must be considered? Eliminating ambiguity on these counts can dramatically increase the quality, speed, and yield of a decision and optimize the effort involved.

Determine the *who*: RAPID®

Even if the decision itself is clear, individuals may be confused about their own roles and responsibilities, just as they were at International Energy.

The approach we have found most practical for defining decision roles and accountabilities is a time-tested method known as RAPID® (figure 4-2). RAPID is a means of analyzing the roles

FIGURE 4-2

RAPID®, a practical tool for allocating decision roles

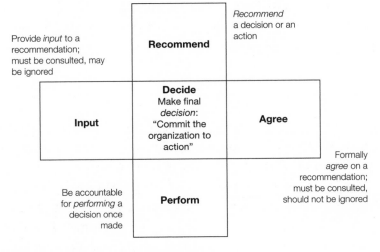

Note: RAPID is a registered trademark of Bain & Company, Inc.

that crop up in every decision. By spelling out the roles that each person or group plays, the tool cuts through the usual ambiguity about who's responsible. It creates a new way of looking at decisions and a new language for discussing them. We have used RAPID since the early 1980s to help hundreds of companies develop clear decision accountabilities. Adopters like the tool because it is intuitive, simple, and designed explicitly for decisions.[1]

The words that form the acronym RAPID—recommend, agree, perform, input, and decide—reflect the primary roles in any decision, though we have taken liberties with the sequence to create a memorable acronym. The roles are described on the following pages.

Recommend

The person in the *recommend* role leads the process. He or she is responsible for obtaining and evaluating the relevant facts and other inputs and then proposing alternative courses of action.

The recommender, naturally, has to have strong credibility both with the decision maker, so that the recommended alternatives carry weight, and with the people responsible for input, so that they feel their contribution will be appropriately evaluated and considered. The recommender typically does most of the work in preparing for any decision.

Input

People with *input* responsibilities provide the relevant facts that are the basis of any good decision. They also offer their own judgments, based on their experience. How practical are the proposals? Are they financially feasible? If dissenting or otherwise contrasting views are likely, the recommender needs to bring the potential dissenters to the table at the right time. The recommender is not obliged to act on the input he or she receives, but is expected to take it into account—particularly since the people who provide input are often among those who must eventually implement the ultimate decision.

Agree

People who must *agree* to a recommendation are those who must sign off on it before it can move forward—executives with legal or regulatory compliance responsibilities, for instance. If they aren't satisfied, they must help the recommender come up with better alternatives or else elevate the issue to a higher level. The agree role, in other words, carries veto power over the recommendation. The recommender can't take a proposal to the decision maker if the people who need to agree are questioning it.

Decide

Eventually, one person will *decide*. (Many RAPID users say that this person "has the D.") The decision maker obviously needs good information, good business judgment, a grasp of the relevant trade-offs, and a keen awareness of the organization that will execute the decision. Giving the D to one individual ensures single-point accountability. As Harry Truman said, the buck stops here. If the decision rests with a committee, the committee should know exactly who in the group is expected to make the decision. For example, the choice could be made by the chair or the senior member, by a majority vote, or by the group as a whole through consensus. (There's more on decision methods in chapter 5.)

Perform

The final role in the process involves the individual or group who will *perform*, or execute, the decision. It's this party's job to implement the decision promptly and effectively. This is a crucial role to assign, so that there's a smooth transition from decision to action. It's also an essential role in the whole decision sequence, since a good decision executed quickly often beats a brilliant decision executed poorly or slowly. Incidentally, people with the responsibility to perform may be valuable in the input role as well, to ensure that decisions are made with execution in mind.

Using RAPID at Intel

Companies can make vast improvements in any given decision simply by spelling out who will play these five roles. Consider the case of Intel's Embedded and Communications Group (ECG).

ECG develops and markets semiconductor devices for a wide range of industrial, automotive, and communications applications. At one point not long ago, the group was struggling with decisions about what should go on its "roadmap" of products slated for development. The general manager and marketing director responsible for each of ECG's three product areas wanted a say. So did ECG's strategic planning manager who looked across all three areas. Because of the confusion, says ECG general manager Doug Davis, "We were making decisions without including the right people, so they didn't stick." Quality and speed both suffered. "Someone who hadn't been involved early on would bring a new piece of data, and we'd go back and revisit the decision."

As part of a reorganization of his unit, Davis and his team used RAPID to define the who for this and other critical decisions. For the roadmap, they gave the D to the strategic-planning manager within ECG, as he was best placed to make trade-offs across ECG's product areas. Implementation wasn't perfectly smooth. Some product general managers, for example, weren't happy with "just" an input role and would second-guess the strategic-planning manager's decisions. But Davis and his team reinforced the new roles, and soon the decisions were going smoothly—and a lot more quickly. "We're not thrashing around on these things as much," says Davis. "We're not going back to revisit decisions that were already made."

RAPID can also clarify roles between an organization's center and its local operations and help push decision making down where appropriate. Consider the case of Boys Town. A well-known youth-services organization in the United States—it was the subject of an Academy Award–winning film in 1938—Boys Town by 2006 had grown into a $200 million organization offering a range of services. But a new executive director, Father Steven Boes, found widespread recognition that the organization was unable to respond quickly, particularly with regard to youth-care services. Boys Town's traditional centralized approach to decisions had served the organization well in the past but now had become increasingly slow and cumbersome. "If a youth-care worker was hired in Las Vegas," one staff member says, "national had to sign off on it." The organization used RAPID to clarify decision authority. If a decision was going to affect the entire organization, such as the addition of a new model component, the vice president of the respective functional department would have the D, regardless of where the decision point originated. Hiring for local expert positions, such as legal counsel or a site development director, would always need an A from the corresponding corporate department. Clarifying these and other roles helped release a new level of energy in the organization and speed up decisions.[2]

Tips for success

Using RAPID effectively takes practice and discipline. Here are some useful rules of thumb:

- *Ensure that only one person has the D.* More than one would-be decision maker is a common ailment among matrix-based organizations. The famous Yahoo! "peanut butter manifesto," a critical screed written in 2006 by a senior executive, complained, "There are so many people in charge (or who believe they are in charge) that it's not clear if anyone is in charge." When Carol Bartz became the CEO of Yahoo! in early 2009, she made it a priority to spell out accountabilities around decision making and execution. She began by making certain that only one member of her team had the D for a given decision.

- *Limit the A roles—and ensure that their sign-off is on the recommendation, not on the decision itself.* Organizations often permit too many vetoes. For decisions to work smoothly and speedily, agree roles should be assigned sparingly. Most important, people in this role should think of their job as determining whether a particular course of action *can* be taken, not as determining whether it *should* be taken. They should withhold agreement only if a proposed alternative would interfere with a course of action being pursued elsewhere in the company or if their expertise indicates it is out of bounds in some other way. In short, anyone in an agree role needs to be involved early in the process—when the recommendation is being shaped, not after it's complete. Veteran RAPID users like to say, "Put the A on the R, not on the D." The point of the A role, after all, is not to second-guess the decision maker, but to ensure that robust recommendations are proposed.

- *It's not just about who has the D!* People can get too focused on who has the decision-making role, perhaps because it implies power. Leaders may need to reinforce that all roles are important. Without good input, for example, decision quality will suffer. Companies that make RAPID work best invest a lot of time in defining all the roles for critical decisions. And these firms ensure that all the key players know their roles—including those who will no longer be involved in a decision.

- *Don't underestimate the role of the person or team responsible for delivering on the decision—the perform role.* Deciding is not the same as delivering. If the link between decision and performance isn't explicit, it's likely to be a source of delay or confusion. To avoid that, top companies always specify who is responsible for performing; they often request input from those people to ensure that implementation challenges are considered in the decision process. These companies also make sure the performer is accountable, even though that individual or group isn't making the decision. Dow, for example, embeds decisions regarding business-unit strategy in performance contracts. The contracts detail the specific strategic decisions that have been made, the resources required to implement the strategy effectively, and who is accountable for delivering on strategy decisions.

- *When necessary, be explicit about who will decide the RAPID roles.* Companies we work with sometimes ask, "Who has the D on 'Who has the D'?" Of course, they are not looking to do a formal RAPID assessment on how to determine decision accountabilities. But in cases where there might be significant controversy, it's good to agree up front on how decisions about roles will be made. And it's wise not to delegate those decisions too far—the decision maker has to feel comfortable with the approach for it to work.

In general, it's important not to go overboard. Explicit RAPID roles need to be created for decisions that merit this level of investment, not for every decision. Intel's Davis says, "We realized right away that there were twelve to fifteen decisions that we rely on to run the business day to day. So we started there." And, of course, RAPID is not a panacea. An indecisive executive in a key role, for instance, can ruin any good system. For RAPID to be effective, it needs the support of all the organizational elements we'll discuss in chapter 5.

Understand the *how*

With the decision defined and the roles clarified, how else can decision making and execution break down? Well, think for a moment about *how* major decisions are made at many companies, maybe even your own. A day or so before the key meeting, you and the other attendees get copies of a 165-page presentation. The presentation outlines the main recommendation, the reasons for it, and all the data that supports it. You probably set the presentation aside, because you know you'll be walked through it at the meeting. Sure enough, the first hour consists of a trip through those 165 slides, complete with voiceover.

When it comes time to make the decision, though, people don't know what to do. Some don't agree with the facts on slides 37 to 42, say. Others believe that the team hasn't looked at the right data. Still others agree with the facts, but favor a different option from the ones examined. For your part, you're fine with the facts and the recommendation—you just don't think there's a reasonable plan to implement the decision.

And that's only one kind of process breakdown. Plenty of other things can obstruct decision processes as well: a lack of coordination with other affected groups, poor communication of decisions, and so on. If any of these obstructions crop up regularly in your organization, you need to improve the *how* of your critical decisions. The key is to follow the five decision disciplines shown in figure 4-3.

FIGURE 4-3

The *how*—elements of a best-practice decision process

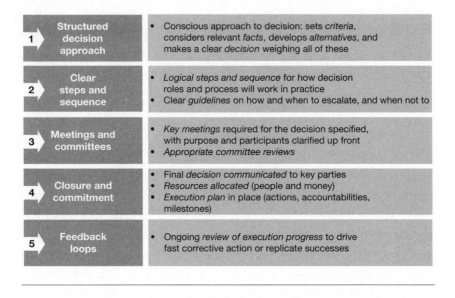

1	Structured decision approach	• Conscious approach to decision: sets *criteria*, considers relevant *facts*, develops *alternatives*, and makes a clear *decision* weighing all of these
2	Clear steps and sequence	• *Logical steps and sequence* for how decision roles and process will work in practice • Clear *guidelines* on how and when to escalate, and when not to
3	Meetings and committees	• *Key meetings* required for the decision specified, with purpose and participants clarified up front • *Appropriate committee reviews*
4	Closure and commitment	• Final *decision communicated* to key parties • *Resources allocated* (people and money) • *Execution plan* in place (actions, accountabilities, milestones)
5	Feedback loops	• Ongoing *review of execution progress* to drive fast corrective action or replicate successes

Use a structured decision approach

Companies that are best at handling decisions use a consistent, well-defined approach for every major decision, whether it is being made in the C-suite or on the front lines. They modify it only to take into account the value that is at stake—more care and attention for high-value decisions, less for lower-value ones. Each company, of course, develops an approach that fits its own circumstances and culture. But the best practices are remarkably similar from one company to another, and many writers, including ourselves, have described them.[3] They typically include the following:

- *Agreement on criteria.* By what yardstick will a decision be evaluated? If the criteria are vague or controversial, decision making and execution slow down. If International Energy's goal had been to maximize revenues, say, then shutting down the T662 would have been a poor choice. But if the company had been seeking to maximize profitability, as was the case, then canceling the product was the best option.

- *All the relevant facts.* A second imperative is to make sure you have the facts you need. Too many decisions are based on gut feel, intuition, or the decision maker's experience, without reference to the relevant data. If there is information, it often arrives too late (an hour before the meeting) or in a form that's too hard to digest (that 165-page presentation). We suspect that the data provided to the COO of International Energy wasn't always of the highest quality. What was the long-term demand for the T662? What were the supplier liabilities?

  Facts always make decision making and execution easier. When CEO Sol Trujillo began work at Telstra, the Australian telecommunications company, in 2005, he and his team needed to make swift decisions about priorities and resource allocation. The challenge was that the company had no agreed-upon fact base for business performance. Key metrics such as the number of fixed-line customers looked different, depending on where the data had come from. Gavan Corcoran, a manager in the transformation program office at the time, remembers that there were many different sources of information, each one supporting a particular "view of the world." Trujillo and his team quickly persuaded the organization to arrive at a common view of the truth. They then used this data to make tough decisions on where to invest and where to prune.

- *More than one real alternative.* It is said that whenever Henry Kissinger, the former U.S. secretary of state, asked his foreign policy team for alternatives, the team would always present three. The first invariably resulted in unconditional surrender to the Soviet Union. The second led to thermonuclear war. The third was always the one the team wanted to pursue. Many executives face the same problem: they don't get good alternatives, so it's hard to make good choices. At IE, the choices seemed to be to discontinue the T662 or not. But had the decision been framed early on as "What should we do to generate the most profit for the business?" there might have been other viable alternatives. The product might have been scaled back, redesigned, or built and marketed through a joint venture. We don't know, of course, because alternative courses of action were never explored. Decision makers need *real* alternatives, preferably more than two, to be able to make the best possible choice.

Like RAPID, a structured decision approach—criteria, facts, real alternatives—has the great advantage that people eventually come to understand it and expect it. If one person isn't following the drill, someone else is likely to raise a red flag. Simple questions like "What alternatives did we consider and reject?" will become part of the leadership dialogue. Before long, it will be second nature—no need for rigid rules or frequent reminders.

Establish guidelines for steps and sequence (including escalation)

Most big decisions require interactions between departments, functions, units, or teams. Intel's ECG, for example, makes frequent decisions involving several product organizations. A good decision process specifies how people in the various groups will play their roles: at what stage they will provide input, when a recommendation will be developed, how approval will be sought when necessary, and how the final decision will be reached. All these steps have to be laid out in a logical sequence, and all the interested parties have to know and understand the process. Just as the life-of-a-decision chart in a decision X-ray can reveal process disconnects, a similar chart in a decision reset lays out how the process *should* work.

Of course, some decisions will encounter intractable disagreement and will have to be escalated. Escalation is one of the thorniest problems any organization faces. Sometimes, too much is escalated; sometimes, too little. The senior executive team of one consumer products company found itself debating the exact shade of blue on a product's label. At ABB, major decisions exposing the company to significant risks weren't always pushed up to someone with a sufficiently broad view.

The most effective companies set clear guidelines about when escalation is appropriate and when it isn't. They define the path that would-be escalators should follow. And they are careful not to shoot the messenger when an executive hears something he or she may not like from people at lower levels. At Intel, where too much was being escalated, Doug Davis recalls, "I set the expectation that we were not going to allow maverick escalations around the process." At the same time, Davis spelled out the path to follow if someone really believed a given approach was "doomed to fail."

Design meetings around specific decisions

With today's managers spending 50 percent or more of their time in meetings, it's surprising how few meetings actually support good decision making and execution. For example, we surveyed executives a few years back and found that about two-thirds of meetings run out of time before participants can make important decisions. Not surprisingly, 85 percent of the executives surveyed were dissatisfied with the efficiency and effectiveness of meetings at their company.[4]

The answer to unproductive meetings isn't to end meetings; it's to design and run them with decisions in mind. As part of defining the how for a given decision, it's worth thinking through which meetings you need to have, who should attend, and what will be accomplished at each one. One technology company, for instance, was trying to improve its decisions about revenue forecasting. Managers realized they would benefit from creating an "interlock" meeting that brought product development and sales together to debate assumptions and decide on revenue targets and account priorities.

With the right meetings identified, the trick is then to run each one to ensure that the objectives are met. At Cadbury, Todd Stitzer and his executive committee met six times a year to review operations and make critical decisions. Materials for those sessions were distributed in advance, with each item marked "Information Purpose Only," "For Discussion and Debate," or "Decision and Action." The taxonomy helped Stitzer ensure that all the items in the last category were addressed.[5]

Close and commit

Ultimately, of course, translating a decision into action requires that people know that a decision has been made; it also requires that resources be allocated or rebalanced to support execution. None of this happened at IE. The COO thought that his decision to cancel the program would stick, but he obviously didn't communicate it forcefully enough for the factory manager to take action. Worse, the resources supporting the manufacture of the T662 weren't allocated away from the program, so the plant was able to continue building turbines as if there had been no cancellation. At Intel, communications was a key part of transforming ECG's product roadmap decisions. Davis says, "We developed a regular cadence of 'Here's what we've done, here's why we've done it' to help people understand what's being added to the roadmap and why. This has reduced the amount of revisiting we do by a lot."

Establish feedback loops

Understanding whether your decision is actually being executed—and getting an early read on whether it was a good decision—can be essential to turning decisions into results. Jim McNerney, CEO of The Boeing Company, once pointed out how simple execution would be "if every second of every day management knew whether they were on plan or off plan and why." The ability to track the execution of decisions and get feedback on results allows managers to take fast corrective action or replicate successes. High performers get close to this ideal by identifying the key metrics, watching them relentlessly, and following up quickly. In 2004, for instance, Wal-Mart Stores decided not to offer steep discounts during the holiday selling season. On the Friday after Thanksgiving—the season's traditional opening day—competitors noticed Wal-Mart's strategy and began trumpeting their own holiday discounts, sensing an opportunity to draw customers away from the retail giant. But Wal-Mart had a robust feedback loop in place, and its executives soon realized their new approach wasn't working. They quickly reversed the decision—and within days, every store in the Wal-Mart system had returned to the company's traditional practice of holiday discounting. Wal-Mart's same-store sales for the month rose 3 percent, not far behind Target's 5 percent, thanks to the leadership's ability to respond quickly to feedback and the organization's ability to swiftly execute the new decision.

Tips for success

Getting the how right is another area where experience makes a big difference. Top performing companies typically follow these practices:

- *Separate the decision from the discussion of choices.* In our experience, organizations try to do too much at once in making decisions. Many leaders look at facts, alternatives, and choices in a single session, for example. This may seem efficient, but more often than not, it leads to analytical shortcuts (limiting decision quality), rework (slowing the pace of a decision), or weak action planning (putting execution at risk). The pharmaceutical company Roche under CEO Franz Humer developed a two-part system for major decisions. People would first consider the relevant facts and proposed alternatives. They discussed whether the facts were sufficient, whether all the right alternatives were on the table, and whether everyone agreed on the criteria for making the ultimate choice. In a separate session, they would then choose from among the alternatives and plan how to mobilize for execution. This two-step process contributed to Roche's superior performance for much of Humer's tenure.

- *Follow the Rule of Seven for meetings.* Who should come to a meeting is always a sensitive issue, and the basic precept is often "The more the merrier." But more is rarely better when it comes to making decisions. Our research highlights what we might call the Rule of Seven: every person added to a decision-making group over seven reduces decision effectiveness by 10 percent. If you take this rule to its logical conclusion, a group of seventeen or more rarely makes any decisions. Of course, a larger group may sometimes be necessary to ensure buy-in. But organizations trying to make important decisions should limit the size of the group as much as possible.

- *Track the timing as well as the level of bottleneck resources to ensure effective execution.* Timing, as they say, can be everything. If performance depends on one particular resource, as it often does, a key measure of execution must capture whether the right level of resource gets to the right place at the right time. So companies must track the level of resources both over time and at specific points in time to ensure performance. A few years ago, for instance, Cisco Systems had decided to roll out a series of products for the rapidly growing Internet protocol (IP) telephony market. Executives came to realize that the number of trained service engineers—people capable of developing new products and applications and training customers in how to use them—was the single most important factor in determining the rate of revenue growth. So the executives closely tracked the hiring, training, and deployment of these engineers in the field, knowing that the measure would give them an accurate, time-sensitive view of execution—in effect, a leading indicator of revenue growth.

These imperatives—simple to implement, but often ignored—help assure the how of decisions. They provide an essential element in the evaluation of any given decision's chances for success. But there's one more dimension required, and that is time.

Make the *when* explicit

While most executives recognize the importance of speed in making and executing decisions, organizations often fail to specify any sort of deadline or timetable for either step. As a result, the pressure is never on. Decisions are postponed, sometimes indefinitely. So is execution. Have you ever sat in meetings where the group agrees to come back to a given topic the next time and thought to yourself, "Can we really afford to wait three more weeks?"

Clear, specific timetables and schedules

The best performers always make the when of decisions explicit. They create schedules, timetables, milestones, deadlines. They ensure that decisions are quickly followed by action, so that things happen rapidly and nobody is tempted to reopen the discussion. Bob Walter, the CEO who led Cardinal Health from start-up to $100 billion in sales during his tenure, was a stickler for avoiding decision drift. He would say, Delay is the worst form of denial. When an issue hit the executive agenda at Cardinal, accordingly, the clock began ticking. Every team had a certain length of time to come back with facts, alternatives, and recommendations. Every executive had a strict timetable for making a decision and seeing that it was carried out.

We recommend to clients that they follow Walter's example and set up an explicit timetable for every critical decision. If you plan to outsource to a Chinese supplier, you should know when you will make the decision, when you expect to identify local business partners, when you plan to receive your first shipment, and so on. The decision timetable should specify the drop-dead date for every major step along the way. Of course, sometimes the best decision is to change the timeline, if a delay will provide better information or improve the competitive lie of the ball. The key is to eliminate unproductive delays in decisions and action.

Tips for success

Again, high performers have come up with several useful tools and techniques to make sure that everyone factors the when into making and executing decisions.

- *For individual decisions, revisit the timetable at the beginning of each meeting.* If a group is responsible for a decision, it should know at every meeting where it stands versus the agreed process and deadlines. To speed up the pace of decisions at Intel, for example, executives regularly review their decision timetable and track their progress in making key decisions on schedule.

- *For groups of interconnected decisions, lay out a "decision drumbeat."* When one major brewer acquired another, team members set an aggressive timeline for integration and stretch targets for synergies and results. To deliver, they mapped out the major decisions required, such as consolidation of manufacturing facilities, distribution channels, and advertising contracts. They then specified all the smaller decisions that had to happen before the major decisions could be made, and the team laid those out on a detailed calendar. Presto: right from the start, there was a drumbeat to keep the integration marching ahead—people knew exactly what was coming up, what information they would need at what time, and so on. Of course, a decision calendar isn't relevant only for acquisitions. It's also useful for any process with many linked decisions, such as strategy development or the launch of a new product.

- *Record when a team "decides not to decide," and strive to reduce this percentage.* Sometimes, not making a decision is the right choice. More often, it's just a way of postponing things for no good reason. If you track these delays, you may be surprised by what you find. One utility company we worked with did this and found that it was postponing decisions 60 percent of the time. So every decision was slow. As the company reduced its "decide not to decide" percentage, it sped up its decision making and execution and reduced the effort for all involved. Not surprisingly, performance improved as well.

Timetables ensure that decisions get made at the right speed and that execution stays on track. If IE had instituted a deadline, the chances of its needing a second decision point, let alone an eleventh, would have fallen dramatically.

Use what, who, how, and when to reset decisions

A decision reset—working through the what, who, how, and when—is a great way to get a critical decision back on track. International Energy could have used one on the T662, thus avoiding all those foul-ups and costs. At least IE's leaders learned from the debacle; once they perceived how much trouble they had with big decisions, they began to work on getting their decisions right. As the pace and quality of decision making and execution picked up, so too did the company's performance.

In chapter 2, we began the story of Hospira, the specialty pharmaceutical and medical device company that sought to increase its effectiveness on many critical decisions. Among those decisions were everyday operational matters such as producing marketing materials. That particular process seemed to take forever. Too often, it didn't lead to good, effective sales aids. So a Hospira team attacked it in just the manner outlined in this chapter.

What

Hospira's first step in the decision reset was to clarify what it was trying to decide. That meant spelling out the goal of the marketing materials. Everybody knew that the U.S. Food and Drug Administration (FDA) had strict regulatory restrictions on what a pharma sales aid could say. But discussions with the team suggested that while the employees were rightly concerned with complying with FDA guidelines, they didn't put enough emphasis on the benefits of the product. So Hospira agreed that the what of the decision process was to develop effective, compelling brochures that were also FDA compliant. This shift in understanding was a critical first step in successfully diagnosing and redesigning the decision.

Who

Next, the team analyzed the current RAPID roles and discovered that decision roles were less than clear. Marketing, regulatory, and medical functions all believed they had the D on decisions regarding sales aids. Once the team established that marketing owned the process, everyone else wanted to have an A, or agree role. Further discussion unbundled the decisions involved and resolved the issue. Regulatory, for instance, was given an A on the words that could be used. Marketing was given the D on most subdecisions (figure 4-4). CEO Chris Begley explains how he hoped RAPID would help keep decisions on track: "If the medical person is giving input on, say, the color, and there's no clinical benefit to making the change, the person who has the D can just say, 'Thanks for your input, but we're moving on.'"

How

The team also addressed the decision process for developing a sales aid. In the existing process, colleagues jotted down comments on a draft and passed it around in a manila folder. Team members received the draft with no context for the critiques and were left to

FIGURE 4-4

Hospira's decisions on marketing materials, before and after RAPID

		Product marketing	Corp marketing and communications	Medical	Regulatory	Creative	Sales/ customer	Global marketing
Before: "What marketing materials will be compliant with FDA regulations?"		R/D	R	D	D	I/P	I	I
After: "What marketing materials will be compelling to customers, while also compliant with FDA regulations?"								
Subdecisions	• Who is the target audience, and what is the message?	R/D				I/P		
	• What words can we use?	D	R	A	A	I/P	I	I
	• What is the look and feel?	D	R	I	I	I/P	I	I

Legend:
- R ecommend
- A gree
- P erform
- I nput
- D ecide

interpret and make their own edits as best they could. Going forward, the team agreed to hold focused meetings to discuss specific issues on a brochure and thereby provide the person in the recommend role with more information and insight. Team members also clarified the criteria by which alternatives would be evaluated. Finally, they identified clear rules for escalation, since the role of decision maker was held almost entirely within marketing. In the rare case that the medical or regulatory teams felt it was necessary to escalate, the head of marketing and the head of either medical or regulatory, or both heads, would take up the issue within forty-eight hours. Hospira didn't expect this to happen often.

When

Finally, the team outlined a timeline for decisions. Each step in the process—determining a promotional strategy, developing a brief, customizing the language, and distributing a draft—got its own deadline. So everyone had clear guidelines as to how long each step and the entire project should take.

The Hospira team redesigned the what and the who of these decisions in a one-day workshop. Colleagues from marketing, regulatory, and medical all attended. Team members collaborated on the how and when over the following weeks. Finally, the entire group met to finalize the process.

The results have been positive. Where the teams used to take about four weeks to approve a sales aid, they are now churning through approvals much faster. Maybe more important, Hospira's marketing, regulatory, and medical teams all feel that the new approach is having a positive impact and that they are having appropriate influence on the decisions. In a survey asking participants to rate their satisfaction along a number of criteria, every question scored at least a 4.5 out of a possible 5. The success of the new approach with this very tangible decision motivated Hospira executives to tackle resets of other major decisions, an effort that is already boosting performance.

Resetting decisions the way Hospira did is a powerful step toward better results. But it often runs into unanticipated obstacles and barriers—which means, usually, that the organization itself is somehow getting in the way. In the following chapter, we'll examine the organizational elements that may be the culprits and help you figure out how to eliminate them.

[5]

Build an Organization
That Can Decide and Deliver

An executive we'll call Kei Arai had a challenge on his hands. An up-and-comer, he had just been assigned to a new project working with the senior team of UD Trucks—formerly Nissan Diesel—on a major transformation. The Japanese truck manufacturer had been acquired by Volvo in 2007, and the new owners were counting on aggressive performance improvements. In the Japanese market, the team had plotted a strategy focused on selling to large, nationwide operators and pursuing growth in profitable after-sales service. But how could the company turn this new strategy into a reality?

One problem was that major decisions weren't working well. Decisions about pricing and service levels for key national accounts, for example, weren't integrated across the network. Each branch set its own policy. Still, just assigning roles and establishing a process for decisions like these wouldn't be enough to put UD Trucks on the road to success. The firm's structure was too complicated. Its one hundred branches were divided into ten regional sales companies, which operated as silos. Then, too, the organization's key performance indicators weren't focused on the right things. The sales staff, for instance, was rewarded mainly on sales volume, with minimal emphasis on anything to do with services. And the culture wasn't yet attuned to a truly integrated national strategy.

Arai knew UD Trucks was facing a major organizational realignment. It would be tough. But he was excited to be part of the team that would address it and help set the company on a path to achieve its ambitious goals.

THE ULTIMATE CHALLENGE for any organization is not just to fix individual decisions as we described in chapter 4. It is to create an environment where best practices happen naturally—where the whole organizational system supports people in making and executing good decisions quickly. To sustain great performance, you have to determine which elements of the organization actually do reinforce good decisions and which don't. Then you can adjust the parts that are getting in the way.

Organizations, of course, are complex entities, and it can be hard to get your mind around all the elements that have to work together successfully to produce great performance. We find it useful to divide the elements into two broad categories, *hard* and *soft*.

The hard elements are those you can write down on paper or can map on a computer screen. The organization has a structure described by the boxes and lines on its organization chart. Individuals have job titles and role descriptions. The organization operates through processes, information flows, and metrics, and it employs a system of incentives. No company can decide and deliver if its structure doesn't fit its purpose, if its roles aren't clearly defined, if its processes don't run smoothly, or if it doesn't have good information and incentives. The hard elements are like an organization's plumbing and wiring. They all have to work right in order for it to function.

The soft elements are different. They relate directly to the human beings who populate the organization. Far from being plumbing or wiring, the soft elements are more like the organization's animating spirit. People, after all, can't be captured in a diagram or defined by a role. They aren't motivated solely by money. They have ambitions and passions, strengths and shortcomings. They have feelings about their work and about how they are treated, and these feelings affect how they act. So organizations succeed not just on the basis of mechanical efficiency but also on the attributes that energize and inspire people—the power of their principles, the strength of their cultures, the alignment and behavior of their leaders. If a company wants to be a top performer, its plumbing and wiring must function properly. But its spirit has to soar.

The elements we include under the hard and soft headings carry familiar names: structure, roles, processes, culture, and so on. Much has been written elsewhere about each of these elements. The difference here is that we're viewing all of them from one unifying perspective—decisions. We'll focus exclusively on what needs to happen in each area to facilitate better decision making and execution. Figure 5-1 shows the difference between the traditional approach and a decision-centered approach. The traditional questions aren't wrong. But when they're phrased in the usual manner, there is no obvious way to tie them together or link them to performance. The decision-centered approach provides the missing link, ensuring that each element of the organizational system supports the decisions that matter most.

The Hard Elements

So let's examine each of the ten decision-oriented questions in the figure. We'll begin with the first five, which relate to the organizational plumbing and wiring. Troubles in any of these hard

FIGURE 5-1

Decision-centered versus traditional approach to organization

	Traditional approach	Decision-centered approach
Hard	Is our structure aligned with our strategy?	Does our structure support the decisions most critical to creating value?
	Who should report to whom?	What are the specific roles and accountabilities for our critical decisions?
	Are our core business processes effective and efficient?	Are our processes geared to produce effective, timely decisions and action?
	Do our information systems support our business objectives?	Do the people in key decision roles have the information they need when and how they need it?
	Is our compensation competitive with peers?	Do our performance objectives and incentives focus people on making the right decisions for the business?
Soft	Do we have a clear and compelling mission and vision?	Do people throughout our organization have the context they need to make and execute the decisions they face?
	Is our management style sufficiently inclusive?	Are our people clear on our preferred decision style (directive, participative, democratic, consensus)?
	Are we winning the war for talent?	Do we put our best people in the jobs where they can have the biggest impact on decisions?
	Do we have an effective leadership team?	Do our leaders at all levels consistently demonstrate effective decision behaviors?
	Do we have a high-performance (sometimes "customer-centric") culture?	Does our culture reinforce prompt, effective decision making and action throughout the organization?

elements—structure, roles, processes, and so on—can obstruct good decision making and execution and can sabotage efforts to reset your critical decisions.

Does our structure support the decisions most critical to creating value?

When an organization isn't functioning smoothly, the first thing many executives look at is its structure. That often seems like the easiest thing to fix, because you can change it with the stroke of a pen. But restructuring can be costly, confusing, and demoralizing. And it often fails to achieve the hoped-for goals. In our experience, many companies can solve their organizational problems through clearer roles, better processes, and so forth—in short, through all the other improvements discussed in this chapter— without major restructuring. Fewer than one-third of companies in our survey said that structure was the most important organizational issue holding them back.

In some cases, however, there's no alternative—structure really is getting in the way of getting things decided and delivered. It acts as a barrier to good decisions and execution rather than as an enabler. Such a situation usually calls for one of two possible solutions.

Align the structure with the definition of the business. Sometimes, a shift in the marketplace, in the basis of competition, or in the company's strategy changes things for an organization. A structure that used to work well enough is now hampering decisions rather than facilitating them and so needs major change. We don't want to get into a detailed discussion of different structures here, because what's needed depends so much on the individual company. But one attribute is indispensable: a company's fundamental structure must reflect the appropriate definition of the business and thus support fast, effective action on critical decisions. UD Trucks, for instance, consolidated its ten regional sales companies into a single national sales group that was better suited to the new integrated strategy.

The story of British Gas, a division of the multinational energy and utility company Centrica, is a particularly compelling example of how restructuring can facilitate better decisions. A few years back, British Gas had ambitious plans for growth. But it also had serious performance issues. Poor customer service was driving away customers. Receivables were going uncollected. The company's new leadership team realized that British Gas was simply too large to be managed as one amorphous whole. The team considered breaking the company into geographical divisions—north, south, east, west. Aside from eliminating some diseconomies of scale, though, the advantages of this kind of reorganization weren't clear.

So British Gas looked instead at the sources of value in its business and identified its most important decisions. One segment of customers used large amounts of gas or electricity and paid regularly through guaranteed direct debits. Decisions that helped the company retain these customers, such as how to handle home moves and how best to offer additional services, were critical for this segment. A second customer segment used less energy and paid regularly through a system of prepayment cards. Here the key decisions related to controlling costs, particularly those associated with processing additional payments and meter reading. A third segment wasn't as consistent in keeping up payments. For this group, the critical decisions related to managing receivables.

Recognizing the different sources of value in each of these segments, Phil Bentley, the managing director, decided that the best way to structure the company was by customer segment. The company could then locate accountability for decisions that directly affected customers, such as service levels, positioning, and product bundling, in the business units. Corporate headquarters focused on non-customer-facing matters such as IT and finance. The alignment of structure and decisions helped British Gas improve its performance significantly. The company reduced customer attrition from about 20 percent to less than 10 percent. Its bad debt fell, and the business began growing for the first time in years.

Simplify complex structures. Many companies don't need to undertake major structural changes. How a company defines and links its business units, functions, and geographies may fit the business definition well enough. But within that structure, many companies face a different problem: unnecessary complexity. They may have too many organizational layers. Their managerial spans— the average number of direct reports per manager—may be unnecessarily small. Dotted-line relationships may be confusing, and working groups may have proliferated. Typically, this kind of complexity grows slowly, with each new step fueled by good intentions. But the result is a hopelessly tangled web, and decisions are the loser.

Cutting through the tangles invariably involves simplification: decreasing the number of layers, increasing managerial spans, and reducing organizational overlays. Simplification may enable a company to reduce its head count and thus save money. But the real benefit lies in decision effectiveness.

A useful tool in this context tracks the number of *decision nodes*—the interfaces between regions, functions, and layers required to make and execute important decisions. Companies can literally identify and count the nodes involved in a major decision. And the teams that do so are often surprised by what they find. As spans decrease and layers increase, the number of decision nodes rises not just arithmetically but geometrically. Every addition to the organization—every new geographic area, every new function, every acquisition—increases the number still further. The proliferation of decision nodes produces a sort of quicksand, trapping decisions in the mire and slowing down activity to a point where it nearly stops. Each decision node introduces a different set of hurdles for new products, business development deals, and even options for reducing costs. Eventually a company that was once lean and nimble finds itself sclerotic and sluggish.

Companies that identify a complexity problem can use decision nodes as a gauge of progress toward simplification. Eliminate so many layers of middle management. Increase spans where possible. Centralize some operations. Then count the decrease in the number of decision nodes. Using this method, some companies have been able to reduce decision nodes by a factor of ten or more, with corresponding improvements in costs, speed of action, and innovation.

What are the specific roles and accountabilities for our critical decisions?

Chapter 4 showed how a decision-roles tool such as RAPID can clarify roles and accountabilities for any given decision. But how can a company incorporate these disciplines into the organizational fabric, so that people understand their roles for every key decision? One option is to run an ever-expanding series of RAPID workshops. Workshops can be helpful, but too many of them are likely to prove distracting. In one *Dilbert* strip, the pointy-haired boss asks his assistant to set up a meeting "to decide how we'll decide on new technologies." The assistant replies, "Do you also need a meeting to decide how you will put together a meeting to decide how to decide things?"

A better method of ensuring that RAPID roles are appropriate, consistent, and intuitive relies on just two imperatives: creating a common vocabulary and establishing broad guidelines about how the organization works.

Create a common vocabulary. This is among the simplest of our organizational prescriptions. Recent Bain research has established that only 10 percent of companies globally use *any* decision-roles tools.[1] So most have no common language at all for discussing who should play what role in a given decision. A few companies go to the opposite extreme. One pharmaceutical manufacturer was using no fewer than seven decision-roles tools in various parts of its organization. In effect, the company was a United Nations with no translators.

We recommend using just one such tool, and we prefer RAPID, which was designed explicitly for decisions. But people will need training in the vocabulary and syntax of RAPID, just as they do when they learn any new language. They must learn what it means to have the role of decision maker, recommender, or any of the other RAPID roles. Once they have the basics down, they can begin to define these roles for the big decisions in which they're involved. Hearing leaders speak the language every day, people will eventually become fluent in it. They'll naturally ask who has the D for this decision, whether they should have an I role in that one, and who has the A for a third one. And everybody else will know what they're talking about.

This kind of common language doesn't help only with big decisions; it also helps people clarify everyday decisions on the fly, without a formal process. "I must be honest—at the beginning, I thought RAPID was another piece of bureaucratic nonsense," says ABB human resources director Gary Steel. But as the organization learned to use the tool, Steel changed his mind: "RAPID has been fundamental in helping this organization operate. I don't know how we would have dealt with some of our issues without it."

Establish accountability guidelines. Executives and managers using RAPID assign specific decision roles to individuals. But which individuals should even come under consideration? Without any guidelines, a global marketing vice president might be torn between giving the D for a particular decision to someone in a country organization and giving it to someone in his or her own function. Without any guidelines, senior leaders might wonder whether IT should call the shots on a new technology solution or whether it should be the business unit that will use the system. In order to assign decision roles effectively across the organization, companies need to define some guiding principles for the roles of business units, global functions, shared services centers, and corporate or regional headquarters. These principles help managers throughout the company know where accountabilities for decisions should sit, bringing simplicity and consistency to RAPID tools and clarifying the roles in hundreds of decisions.

There is no formula that suits every situation. Each company has to develop guidelines that match its business definition, management philosophy, culture, and strategic objectives. British American Tobacco's guidelines, for instance, reflected the need to balance strong global roles in key areas such as brand management and procurement with strong local autonomy in execution. This simplifying approach spelled out a logic for decision accountabilities and guided how individual decisions throughout the business should work, even where RAPID had not been formalized.

Boys Town, the U.S. youth services organization, also found accountability guidelines helpful. After several months of working through a number of individual decisions with senior leaders, Father Steven Boes and his team proposed a corporate decision matrix to the top one hundred managers. The matrix guidelines codified the various categories of decisions made at Boys Town and mapped out which positions would have authority for each. Decisions covered included HR-related issues, budgets and signing authority, organizational policies, program components and development, property acquisition, and legal issues. Barb Vollmer, project leader of Boys Town's decision initiative, says, "You don't have to write down every decision, because rules emerge after a while. What you are doing with RAPID is capturing the concept so people can understand that *this* kind of decision falls into *that* category."[2]

Are our processes geared to produce effective, timely decisions and action?

Most companies spend a lot of time and effort engineering (and reengineering) their management and business processes. But they often do so without much attention to the decisions involved in each one. Organizations need an explicit link between business processes and decisions. You can see the importance of such a link both with strategic decisions and with everyday operating decisions.

Ensure that strategic planning leads to strategic decisions. Asked what process their company uses to make strategic decisions, most executives say "strategic planning." Ironically, strategic planning at many companies actually leads to few timely, high-quality strategic decisions. Indeed, the traditional planning model is so out of sync with the way executives want and need to make decisions that top managers often sidestep the process when making their biggest strategic choices.

We see two common problems. First, companies develop strategic plans on a predetermined calendar, typically fact gathering in the spring, forecasting in the summer, senior management review and approval in the fall, and budgeting in the winter. But executives must make strategic decisions continuously, whenever market or competitive conditions warrant. The calendar problem is compounded by a second challenge, which we call the business-versus-issue bias. Traditional planning focuses on creating an aggregate plan for a given business, not on teeing up the specific decisions necessary to generate better results. (Should we enter China? Should we buy our distributor? Should we outsource manufacturing? and so on.) Since executives typically make decisions issue by issue, planning by business often produces plans that are little more than summaries of important decisions made elsewhere, rather than a source of any new decisions and actions.[3]

Some top performers, however, have changed all this. Microsoft, Roche, and Dow, for instance, have moved from a business-by-business to an issue-by-issue approach in recent years. Microsoft lists its major issues as "strategic themes" at the beginning of the year, thus clarifying the major decisions the company intends to make as part of its planning process. Roche, the Swiss pharmaceutical company, summarizes its outstanding issues in a strategic agenda and then resolves them continuously throughout the year. Dow uses twenty-to-thirty-year "megatrends" to identify major strategic issues and opportunities, a process that has significantly enhanced the company's ability to formulate long-term strategy options. CEO Andrew Liveris told us, "We can now see how our portfolio stacks up with where the true growth opportunities are, and allocate scarce capital and technical resources to drive profitable growth." In all of these cases, the calendar-driven, business-unit-focused model is broken down into discrete, decision-focused pieces with specific timeframes. The result for these companies has been a dramatic improvement in the quality and pace of decision making.

Align everyday business processes with decision processes. Every company has a set of business processes that are also critical to its operations. By now it is well understood that these processes need to be focused on the customer and must be lean, continuously improving, and so on. Not so well understood is that even the best business processes can break down if the decision processes that go along with them aren't clear and aligned.

For example, at the Internet company Yahoo!, new-product launches are critical to the company's growth. Every new product, such as a new version of the home page or e-mail, moves through well-defined processes: Yahoo! people develop the product, market it to advertisers and users, launch it, and eventually make sure it operates effectively. But the company was routinely failing, in the words of CEO Carol Bartz, to create "kick-ass" products. What was happening, though, wasn't a failure in the company's business processes; it was a lack of alignment between business and decision processes.

Like many companies, Yahoo! had designed its business processes without clearly laying out the critical decisions that needed to be made across its many functions and regions. Each area would run its own process, but the decisions involved weren't coordinated with those of other functions down the line. So product development might consider a new product finished, even though the regions hadn't yet weighed in on the degree of flexibility needed to meet local user needs, and even though the company's sales organization might not have lined up enough premium advertisers to make it successful. The lack of coordination meant that the end product was often late and lackluster.

Working to remove the blockages, team members carefully defined where the new-product development process stopped and the marketing process began. That helped ensure that decisions were coordinated and balls weren't dropped. They did the same for marketing and sales and other interfaces. Clearly thinking through the link between business processes and decisions enabled Yahoo! to accelerate the pace of new-product introductions and improve its products' appeal to users and advertisers.

Do the people in key decision roles have the information they need when and how they need it?

The world these days is swimming in information. So are most large organizations. But when an individual needs to make a decision, he or she needs only the information directly relevant to that decision. And there's the rub. The right information may be buried in an avalanche of extraneous data or conflicting reports.

It may be available next week rather than right now. Sometimes it's hidden in another function or another level of the organization. ("Someone in the company has surely done this before—but who?")

Cracking these issues is essential. You can't have good, fast decisions and execution without information in the right place at the right time. You need the facts and analyses that are relevant to a given decision, including robust financial analysis; recent performance data; customer, market, and competitor information; and even what has been learned somewhere else in the company from similar situations.

Tailor information flows to decisions. The key to gathering the right information is to think through exactly what is required for critical decisions and to figure out how to make it available in a systematic way. This kind of decision-driven view allowed a natural resources company we worked with to streamline its management reports from five hundred data points to just fifty. A similar approach helps Boeing's Commercial Airplanes division (BCA) match its information collection to the value of each decision. BCA gathers voluminous, detailed information on airline traffic patterns, passenger needs, and competitor offerings before it makes any decision to develop a wholly new commercial airplane program. But it doesn't collect as much information for decisions about derivative aircraft programs, because those decisions don't carry as much value.

Other companies are finding ways to solve the problem of internal information flows. Software company Intuit, for instance, uses a tool called Intuit Brainstorm. This tool allows people to weigh in on any innovation decision on which they have relevant information, regardless of their job titles or positions in the organizational hierarchy. Engineers faced with design decisions, for instance, can gather input from people in finance, strategy, operations, or anywhere else. Brainstorm has helped Intuit increase the number of new ideas discussed by a factor of ten and the number of people actively involved in innovation by a factor of five. The tool also helped the company raise the number of new-product releases from five or six a year to more than thirty, and to decrease the average time required for each one from about thirteen months to less than four. Intuit has even brought some projects, such as ViewMyPaycheck, from conception in Brainstorm to commercially viable products in less than three months.

Create systems designed for decisions. A decision-driven view also helps prioritize investments in information systems and analytics. Today's information technology—from massive enterprise resource planning (ERP) systems and executive dashboards to blogs and wikis—can provide endless amounts of data. But the real issue is what information people need to make and execute critical decisions.

Lafarge's Aggregates & Concrete Division, under executive vice president Tom Farrell, for instance, realized that some of its most important decisions involved managing its fleet of heavy mobile equipment, which was scattered across 620 sites in twenty-five countries. Farrell knew that many decisions relating to the equipment were best made locally. But he also knew that a group with Lafarge's reach should be able to take advantage of its collective knowledge to make and execute better decisions and to better leverage its bargaining power with suppliers through worldwide negotiations.

With that in mind, Farrell invested in a system that captured information about equipment at each site—the location of individual machines, usage levels, maintenance logs, and so on—and married that data with a standard analytic process reflecting group best practices. This system allowed local managers to make better-informed decisions about the size of their fleets, maintenance schedules, and equipment sharing between sites. It allowed the divisional center to be more effective in negotiating global purchasing contracts with manufacturers. Thanks to the new system, Lafarge registered double-digit improvements in key metrics such as the total cost of ownership over the life cycle of the equipment. The company has gone on to develop systems and analytic capability in other critical areas, such as land management. More than 2,300 sites are now covered by Lafarge Aggregates' land information system, enabling local entities to manage land and mineral resources more efficiently and giving the group a unique lever to improve its decisions on critical resources.

Make the information simple, accurate, timely, and accessible. Information that meets these criteria can help produce fast, high-quality decisions. Take Dow. In 2003, when Andrew Liveris became COO, Dow was in the depths of a chemicals recession. Feedstock costs were increasing while end prices were in free fall. To turn the company around, Liveris focused his senior leadership team on quick decision making and execution. Team members defined a simple set of data, including unit prices, input costs, and plant utilization, and shifted tracking from monthly to weekly. They met every Monday to discuss the prior week's performance. These weekly reviews soon became part of the operating rhythm of the company. Executives got used to monitoring key performance data on a close-to-real-time basis and taking quick action to keep the company on track. Thanks partly to these moves, Dow outperformed many of its competitors during this period.

Do our performance objectives and incentives focus people on making the right decisions for the business?

Well-run companies typically translate company goals and metrics into performance objectives for individual managers and employees. Then the companies hold these managers and employees accountable for delivering on their objectives. Here we'll suggest just two actions to ensure that objectives and incentives truly support effective decisions.

Tie objectives and incentives to sources of value. Sometimes, individual objectives and incentives aren't aligned with a business's strategy or sources of value. UD Trucks' sales force, for example, was rewarded mainly on the number of trucks sold in a given period, with only a small incentive for after-sales services. To ensure that incentives helped sales reps make the right decisions about their time and their interactions with customers, the company added new targets for truck inspections (a leading indicator of service revenue) and service profits. This focus helped UD Trucks weather the 2008–2009 downturn better than competitors: it compensated for falling sales volumes with greater service revenue, keeping the operation profitable.

Link a significant portion of objectives and incentives to shared goals. Another common problem is that different organizational units may have conflicting objectives. This may fuel healthy debate, or it may lead to decision gridlock. A large commercial bank we worked with, for instance, was organized by product—credit, cash management, and so on. Relationship managers often drew on many products to meet the needs of the bank's largest customers. But since relationship managers were rewarded on revenues and product managers on profitability, conflict arose any time the relationship manager wanted to use one product as a loss leader to help sell other products.

Creating incentives around shared goals can often resolve this kind of problem. As part of its turnaround, ABB put everyone eligible for a bonus on a plan tied to a group scorecard; the scorecard measured the company's progress on revenue growth, return on capital, and other market-facing metrics. Not everyone liked it at first, says Gary Steel, but ultimately, it "brought a greater degree of alignment." Telstra, similarly, had to change the incentives for its call-center agents. Before, agents had an incentive to minimize the time spent on the phone. But service technicians in the field often got inadequate information from the agents and so were unable to resolve problems on the first visit. The company changed its incentives so that the agents would spend more time on a call, helping customers resolve the issue themselves or else gathering all the information required for a first-visit fix.

While incentives can play a role in attracting and retaining key talent, we don't subscribe to the view that paying people more will necessarily get them to make better decisions. But incentives do affect people's decisions about where to focus their effort and how to make specific trade-offs. Nonmonetary rewards, of course, can be just as important as monetary ones. People value public recognition, training, promotions, expanded job responsibilities, and so on, as well as (and often more than) money. This is particularly true of people who enjoy focusing their efforts on critical decisions—the kind of people you want in your organization.

The Soft Elements

The soft side of the organization is its animating spirit. It's all the intangibles that get people fired up, engaged, and eager to help the organization achieve its goals.

These soft elements are more important than ever in our global, knowledge-based economy. Most people today have jobs that require a good deal of skill and judgment. That's as true of frontline workers as it is of the managers and technical specialists in the higher echelons. Organizations can no longer rely on simple job descriptions to tell employees what to do; nor can they afford to supervise people from minute to minute. On the contrary, it's often the employees themselves who know better than anyone else how to do their jobs.

So nearly every organization must somehow inspire people to do those jobs conscientiously, to collaborate effectively, and to make and execute the many decisions entrusted to them in a manner that furthers the organization's objectives. But to work well on their own, people need to know what's expected of them, and they need to feel involved and engaged. They have to respect and trust their leaders and colleagues and feel fairly treated. They must believe, in short, that the organization functions well, that they want to be a part of it, and they want to give it what Gareth Williams, human resources director of Diageo, calls their "discretionary energy."

From an organization's point of view, achieving all of that depends on good answers to the following five questions.

Do people throughout our organization have the context
they need to make and execute the decisions they face?

In a perfect managerial world, every employee would act like an owner or a CEO. Employees would always do things that were in the best interests of the organization. They would balance the short and the long term. They would stick to the rules when it was required and bend them when that was the right thing to do. Many well-run small businesses work pretty much this way. Employees are close enough to the boss and to one another to know what to do in any given situation. In large organizations, this level of knowledge is harder to attain. Many big companies don't create a clear context for all the decisions an employee must make and execute. They don't define their priorities specifically enough to allow people to make trade-offs. The result is that no one is sure what to do. At one pharmaceutical company, for instance, plant managers kept bumping decisions about manufacturing technology up to senior executives. These middle managers had to do so, because they had no way of knowing whether they should invest in new technologies that could improve cost and performance but could also introduce some regulatory risk.

Build an organization-wide context for decisions. There are plenty of techniques that organizations use to fill this gap. Mission and vision statements, if done well, can help. So can letters from the corner office, corporate mottos (such as Ford's Profitable Growth for All), and communications programs. The key for leaders is to create a context that is inspiring yet sufficiently specific to guide daily actions, to repeat it over and over, and to act in ways that reinforce this context rather than undermine it. As Netflix tells its employees, "The best managers figure out how to get great outcomes by setting the appropriate context, rather than by trying to control their people."

That's essentially what Martin Broughton and his team did at British American Tobacco. The goal of becoming number one in the industry again was itself an inspiring new context for a company that had hitherto focused on internal as well as external competition. The company established a very few priorities to help people make daily trade-offs as they strived to live up to this challenge. For instance, the new focus on growth in premium global brands allowed people to worry less about local value brands. The new emphasis on achieving savings through global scale in procurement encouraged them to seek out suppliers capable of delivering those savings. The rallying cry of "One BAT" reinforced the collaborative message; gone were the days of "warring tribes."

Broughton and his team brought 140 of the company's top leaders together in a three-day conference to kick off the new approach. That alone generated enormous enthusiasm—his closing speech received an eight-minute standing ovation. The senior team then led a series of regional and functional conferences and sent videos explaining the changes to BAT's operations in more than seventy countries. Team members followed up with regular e-mail updates and other sustained communications. Soon it was hard to find a BAT employee who didn't understand the impact of the new priorities on day-to-day decisions and actions. "I think people understand what they need to do much better," says Paul Adams, who was then a regional director in one of the operating units and is now BAT's CEO. "If you have a Kenyan brand manager who has to make a trade-off, you'd expect now that he would choose a course of action knowing that that is what the company wants him to choose. People understand the values and what is expected of them." David Crow, who had been a regional marketing executive with the BATCO division, sums it up this way: "Finally there was a single vision—one team, one leadership, one way."

Are our people clear on our preferred decision style (directive, participative, democratic, consensus)?

Few people in the command-and-control organizations of the last century ever wondered about the right way to make decisions. If you held a position in the hierarchy, you issued orders. Those below you carried them out. Today, many companies have moved away from that directive style to a more collaborative approach. In most ways, this is a good thing: broader participation can improve decision quality and build the buy-in necessary for effective implementation. But the shift has created challenges. Some companies veer too far toward consensus, which can slow down decisions. Others take a laissez-faire approach, allowing managers to pick whatever style works best for them. Agreeing on a common style for how decisions should be made and executed helps decision effectiveness enormously, making it easier to assign roles and ensure appropriate behaviors. So we suggest that organizations follow two precepts.

Select a predominant decision style, and make it work well. Over the years, we have adopted a model that includes four styles—directive, participative, democratic, and consensus. The *directive* style is much like the traditional command-and-control approach: one person has decision authority, and everyone else goes along. The *participative* style also assigns one person the decision-making role, but expects this individual to consult with others who have relevant knowledge or experience. A *democratic* style relies on forms of voting, while a *consensus* style assumes that all involved must reach agreement.

Organizations can often boost decision effectiveness by agreeing on one style to be used in most situations. This reduces ambiguity and helps people focus on best practices for that particular style. Of course, some decisions may require a different style from the norm. If a nuclear power plant is malfunctioning, a directive approach may be appropriate. If a company is choosing which charities to support, a democratic style may be best. The idea is not to be rigid about the approach, but to create a shared understanding of the norm and a way to talk about it when a different style is needed.

Consider using a participative style, which generally works best. We find compelling evidence from both research and experience in favor of the participative style. When MetLife shifted toward this style, CEO Rob Henrikson commented in a video created for internal use,

"The participative style fits well with our desired culture, emphasizing both accountability and collaboration." The same will be true for many high performers: in our survey, more than half of the companies in the top quintile of decision effectiveness said they use mainly a participative style. Employee engagement is also significantly higher in companies with a participative style. Employees of participative companies are three times more likely than other employees to recommend their organization as a place to work.

Changing to a participative style can improve both the speed and the quality of decisions. One pharmaceutical company we worked with moved from a consensus style to participative; the move cut the time required for many of its product launch decisions by reducing the number of meetings and iterations previously required to achieve agreement. Boeing's shift to a participative style under Alan Mulally helped the company improve the quality of its pricing decisions. Its previous directive style excluded information from lower-level executives—input that would have led to better choices.

Your decision and organizational scorecards will indicate if your company has a style that is both generally accepted and effective. If you need to change, recognize that it may not be easy— you have to engage leaders throughout the business on what this change really means in practice, and then you have to follow through. We'll return to this in our discussion of leadership behaviors later in the chapter.

Not every company will need to adjust its decision style. Things may work well enough today. But where ambiguity or an otherwise ineffective style is getting in the way for a company, a conscious choice about decision style and the behaviors it entails helps to lay the groundwork for defining clear roles and processes.

Do we put our best people in the jobs where they can have the biggest impact on decisions?

Many organizations spend a lot of time and money installing state-of-the-art people systems and HR processes. But these groups are often frustrated with the outcomes, because the new procedures don't always have a measurable impact. A decision-focused approach allows executives to look at people policies differently. They can ask which jobs have the greatest impact on their organization's critical decisions and whether the right people are in those jobs.

Identify key positions. Executives have traditionally assumed that the corporate hierarchy reflects a job's importance, and so they focus on the top twenty-five or hundred slots. But what you want to know isn't who ranks the highest; it's which positions have the most impact on important decisions. These positions might be anywhere in the organization—finance, sales, operations, wherever. Some will be frontline supervisors. For instance, a small high-end retailer in the northeastern United States found that its sales associates were the key to higher sales and customer satisfaction. While its competitors focused mainly on goods selection and in-store merchandising, the company invested heavily in information systems designed to help each associate respond more effectively to individual customer needs. This focus on frontline employees enabled the retailer to expand profitably to other locations. When you walk into one of the company's stores today, the sales associate has your purchase history, your tastes, even your spouse's birthday at his or her fingertips.

Put the right people in the right positions. With key positions identified, you need to know which people have the necessary skills to fill them. The management writer Jim Collins has famously said that every company needs to get the right people on the bus and the wrong people off the bus. We agree, of course, but it's equally important to get the right people in the right seats, especially when it comes to mission-critical positions. It's essential to consider decision abilities as part of this mix. Does an individual have the capability to make good decisions in a timely fashion and set up prompt, effective execution? Does he or she demonstrate behaviors consistent with good decisions? Decision competencies can be included in the leadership standards that guide evaluation and deployment.

Assessing these attributes is especially important now, as today's organizations often require a different set of skills than those needed in the past. Work is more collaborative. Decision accountabilities are distributed more widely. As Sandy Ogg, Unilever's chief human resources officer, remarks, "In the old world, we needed a lot of independent four-hundred-meter runners. Today, we need a four-by-one-hundred relay team."

Once you know your critical positions and your top performers, you can make sure there is a match. One technology company, for example, found that a decision-centered approach fundamentally changed how managers thought about talent deployment. First, the company identified its mission-critical positions and assessed how many of these positions were filled by top performers. The answer was less than 30 percent. When the company then asked how many of its top performers were in mission-critical positions, the answer was only 40 percent. Thinking about deployment from a decision perspective helped this company make the most of its talent pool and improve decision effectiveness. The benefits of getting the right person in the right job can be profound. Glenice Maclellan, who until recently was a senior executive in Telstra's Consumer and Channels organization, says, "There is nothing more rewarding than seeing the right person in the right job with the right accountability. They just blossom. There's an opportunity to run faster than ever before."

Do our leaders at all levels consistently demonstrate effective decision behaviors?

Leaders at any level set the tone for how decisions are handled. But some people may agree that decision effectiveness is a priority and then fail to walk the talk. They may second-guess or countermand assigned decision makers. They may make snap decisions without adequate information. At companies that rank high in decision effectiveness, leaders avoid these traps. About three times as many survey respondents from these companies "strongly agree" that their leaders consistently demonstrate behaviors that support good decision making and execution.

Define the desired behaviors. A company looking to boost its decision effectiveness has to be crystal clear about what it expects of leaders. Most organizations ask their leaders to stick to agreed-on decision roles and processes and to seek the best overall answer for the business, not just their own individual part of it. (This last requirement was a huge change for ABB; personal and territorial concerns had dominated decisions for years.) They expect leaders to rely on facts first and judgment second and to welcome open and constructive debate. Once a decision is made, leaders need to follow through with prompt, effective action, without any second-guessing or hoping the decision will simply go away. When he was CEO of Gillette, Jim Kilts noticed that there was a lot of hallway chatter after meetings and that some executives were passively resisting decisions made in those meetings. So he asked his team to agree to a specified code of behaviors, including open and honest debate during a discussion and wholehearted support for the decision once made.[4]

This kind of definition is especially needed when companies are trying to shift from one decision style to another. Changing from consensus to participative is particularly challenging. In this case, a person assigned a decision-making role will need to step up and take it on—often difficult for someone accustomed to relying on consensus. Those who don't have the D need to learn to support the decision, regardless of whether they agree. When people who used to be involved in a decision are no longer part of it, a key behavior is refraining from getting involved and instead trusting others to do a good job. When MetLife was undergoing this change, Bill Mullaney, then president of the company's Institutional Business segment, told his leadership team to "get comfortable with being uncomfortable" at not being involved in every decision.

Support people in changing their personal behaviors. Being clear about what behaviors are needed is one thing; changing behaviors is quite another. People have to hold themselves and their peers accountable for living the behaviors day in and day out. Workshops can help people discuss what the behaviors really mean, learn how to recognize them, and give permission to call one another out when they don't live up to the standards. Some groups pick out the three or four desirable behaviors that are the most challenging for them as individuals. Team members then commit to act as role models in the company by adopting these behaviors. (One tech company even instituted a five-minute behavior check at the end of key meetings.) Of course, some people need more help than this, so 360-degree feedback and coaching on the new behaviors are often critical ingredients of lasting change. Compensation can help, too. At Gillette, executives received four separate annual ratings on their behaviors, one from themselves, one from peers, one from direct reports, and one from then-CEO Kilts. The score affected a meaningful portion of their bonus pay.[5]

Instilling the leadership behaviors necessary for decision effectiveness is essential in and of itself; it is also one of the most important factors in creating an even more fundamental change, a shift in the entire culture of the organization.

Does our culture reinforce prompt, effective decision making and action throughout the organization?

Often, lasting improvements in decision effectiveness require changing a company's culture. Veteran executives know this and don't shrink from it. "Everything we have done has been about a cultural change," says the CEO of one global company mired in complexity. "We've heard it said that a loose definition of culture is what people do when no one is watching. If so, the ideal is for people to make and execute good decisions quickly and routinely, as part of 'the way we do things around here.'"

What are the ingredients of such a culture? One is a unique identity—the specific combination of values, heritage, and ways of working that gives each company its distinctive feel. DaVita, a $5 billion health-care services company, sees itself as "a community first and a company second," and CEO Kent Thiry calls himself mayor of the DaVita village. Southwest Airlines employees often think of their company as a family. One employee says, "We all work hard, but to do anything else would be like letting your family down." As these examples show, the unique identity makes the organization a special place to work and engages employees with the mission. Of course, this organizational personality needs to be complemented by a performance orientation. A top performer typically encourages high aspirations in its employees. It expects them to think like owners and to take an external focus in making decisions. These and similar values are central to decision effectiveness.

Define the culture you want. In strengthening or rebuilding its culture, an organization must show that decisions and action are valued. At Telstra, one of the pillars of the company's push for cultural change in recent years was a sense of urgency, often described as *done.now*. Andrea Grant, Telstra's HR director, explains how it worked: "People would say, 'If we need twenty-seven approvals, that is not *done.now*.' They'd question how to change the way we do things." Kraft Foods, Inc., is another example. Building on its "rewire" strategy, which restructured the company to facilitate growth, Kraft Foods has begun to focus on creating a high-performing organization. A key ingredient is its values, which CEO Irene Rosenfeld believes can inspire an emotional connection between employees and organization. "Pairing our new purpose with clear values unifies employees and enables a high-performing culture," she says. Kraft Foods has developed a list of seven "values in action," each closely tied to performance. The one we like best: "We discuss. We decide. We deliver."

Build a culture that supports decisions. Creating a culture, of course, involves far more than simply agreeing on a list of values. Often, change is required in all the organizational levers that we have discussed in this chapter—clarifying roles, installing better processes, and so on. When each of these organizational elements is working right—when each supports fast, effective decisions and execution—it contributes to an overall culture in which decisions flourish. In short, culture transformation is critical for decision effectiveness, but often a focus on decision effectiveness is itself a major catalyst for culture change. Either way, the result should be a company whose every employee, from the front line to the corner office, can make and deliver great decisions day in and day out.

The role of culture in supporting decision effectiveness is easiest to see when the culture helps generate truly outstanding results, as in the example of Shinhan Bank. Shinhan Bank was founded by Japanese businessmen of Korean descent who sensed banking opportunities in their motherland. At the time, all Korean banks were run by government appointees, whose success was determined by whom they knew as much as by what they delivered. As the first commercial bank in Korea established by a nongovernmental entity, Shinhan vowed to be different.

Shinhan focused its culture on customer satisfaction, adopting the slogan "Becoming a bank that the customers really want to bank with." Its hiring, performance evaluation, and compensation were all based on capability and performance rather than on educational or regional backgrounds. It delegated significant decision responsibilities to lower-level employees who, management knew, often had the best view of the customer. Budding middle managers were expected to spend substantial parts of their careers working in branches and thus interacting directly with customers. Training helped develop the new approach. Baek Soon Lee, bank president and CEO, says, "Intensive training courses help new hires come out of their shells and grow their passion. Such a customer-centric culture is an invaluable asset unique to Shinhan, which other banks can't match."

Shinhan also expected different kinds of behaviors from its employees than those encountered at conventional Korean banks. "Of course, it is time-consuming and sometimes frustrating," says Group CEO Sang Hoon Shin, describing his preference for letting people speak their minds. "However, if I let team members know my thoughts up front, they will be tempted to blindly follow them and will be biased against other possibilities. As a leader of this organization, I feel one of my roles is to create an environment where the best possible ideas are aired out, regardless of who says them." Raising objections against seniors' opinions is not only tolerated, but also expected at Shinhan. And it helps ensure better decisions.

The result of all this is a passion for the business and for customers, which pervades the organization and translates into great decisions at every level. In 1982, Shinhan was ranked number twenty-three in size among Korean banks. In a little more than twenty years, it grew to be the second largest in the industry, and it consistently earns top marks for customer satisfaction.

Conclusion

This chapter has highlighted how a focus on decisions can help you move beyond conventional approaches to organization in ten areas. Any particular organization is likely to find some of the practices we discussed more relevant than others in building an organization that supports effective decisions. For Kei Arai and the team at UD Trucks, the list included structural change, resetting measures and incentives, establishing a clearer context, and building a culture that focused on nationwide success. These moves allowed the company to make and execute the decisions essential to achieving its goals and to deliver a multimillion-dollar annual improvement in operating income. Some companies will need to make changes at least as profound as those at UD Trucks. Others will need just a few tweaks to shore up one or two organizational elements. Whatever the situation, leaders need to make a deep commitment to building and maintaining an organization that supports decision effectiveness, and they must be willing to confront challenges, wherever these challenges may appear. And the focus can't just be on optimizing each individual organizational element. All the elements must work together to reinforce great decision making and execution.

The payoff of doing all this is substantial. An organization aligned on all these different dimensions is an organization that can decide and deliver. And that's what determines performance. High performance as defined by decision effectiveness is not just a buzzword; it leads to consistently outstanding results and creates an organization that people find rewarding to work for—in all sorts of ways.

[6]

Embed Decision Capabilities

Maria Morris, executive vice president of MetLife's Tech-nology & Operations division, looked out at the sea of faces in the audience. The five hundred leaders in front of her would all need to play key roles in the organization's journey to improve decision making and execution. They had to rally around this companywide effort and be ready to drive the change. Most important, they had to be will-ing to do things differently.

They had a lot to be proud of, she told them. MetLife had a track record of making good decisions and execut-ing them well. But as the decision scorecard showed, the company had an opportunity to ratchet up its effective-ness a couple of notches, especially on speed. "Improved decision making is game changing," she said. Better, faster decisions and execution would make MetLife more com-petitive as it reengineered its operations, deepened its relationship with customers, and expanded into global markets.

Morris could see that people were getting fired up. But would they be ready to do everything she was asking? "We are counting on all of you. The path to transforming ourselves into a decision-driven organization will require commitment and tenacity. It will require new skills, new behaviors, and new ways of working that will sometimes feel uncomfortable. Every individual will have to be open to change." The effort to improve decision making and execution couldn't be seen as just another chore—people were already working hard on so many fronts. "Decision effectiveness is not another initiative," she said firmly. "It is a capability—a capability that will help us deliver the initiatives our future depends on. Let's get started!"

The energy in the room was palpable. People clapped loudly and headed off to breakout rooms. There, they would plunge into the learning process, beginning with X-raying some of their own decisions. Technology & Operations—a five-thousand-employee organization that was a critical part of MetLife's business—was on its way.

THE PREVIOUS CHAPTERS have mapped out a plan of attack, a way of diagnosing and addressing decision difficulties. Following the plan, an organization can rid itself of internal logjams and get things decided and delivered. But most organizations have enormous amounts of inertia. It takes time to change them. Without continued effort, they're likely to snap back into the old ways of doing things. If you want decision effectiveness to be more than a four-month flash in the pan, you'll need to embed the new ways of working in your organization and ensure that they produce lasting results. In this chapter, we'll suggest some paths to success and some potholes to avoid along the way.

This fifth step in our program is a little different from the others. It's last in the sequence we have laid out, to be sure. But like any attempt to reshape an organization, you really have to think about the change process from the very beginning (figure 6-1). Which leaders will you count on to spearhead the effort? How will you persuade everyone of its importance? How will you maintain momentum and overcome the obstacles? Ultimately, it is people throughout the organization who will have to make it happen—who will create the capabilities that make for a smoothly running, high-performing, decision-focused company. As Maria Morris knew, how you plan and lead this journey makes the difference between success and failure.

Every company's challenge, of course, is different. Some well-functioning organizations may require no more than a focused effort in a few areas—clarifying roles, say, or establishing better processes for a handful of decisions that aren't working as well as they should. Other companies may need to transform their organization more fully, altering structures, measures, incentives, and other systemic elements. That's a bigger effort and will naturally take more time, resources, and engagement. The trigger for addressing decision effectiveness will also differ from one organization to another, which means that both the context for change and the level of urgency can vary significantly. Some companies

FIGURE 6-1

Five steps to improving decision effectiveness

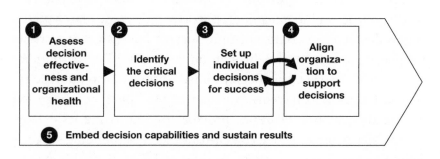

may have gone through a merger or reorganization; some may have new leaders or a new strategy; some may simply feel competitors nipping at their heels and realize they themselves can outstrip rivals by making better decisions, making them faster, and executing more effectively.

Given all these differences, we can't offer a single roadmap. But we have worked with many organizations that have set out on this path. We have seen what has helped them and where they have stumbled. Here we'll summarize this experience in three prescriptions, each one essential to the task of creating lasting results:

- Building the foundation for effective decisions

- Creating and sustaining momentum

- Embedding decision behaviors and capabilities

Each of these prescriptions has its own must-dos for success.

Building the foundation for effective decisions

They say that every journey begins with a single step. Maybe so, but before anybody hits the road, you need to persuade people that the trip is worth taking, that the view is worth the climb, and that the colleagues they most respect are already lacing up their shoes.

Make decision effectiveness a priority

The process has to begin with a powerful rationale for embarking on the journey: a big, meaningful, worthwhile goal. Alan Mulally believed that Ford could not only survive but also recapture its former greatness. Martin Broughton wanted BAT to be number one in its industry. Chris Begley aimed to turn in top-quartile results at Hospira. Rob Henrikson wanted MetLife to be recognized as a leading global insurance provider by improving its performance, sharpening its focus on customers, and expanding successfully in international markets. And Doug Davis at Intel hoped to turbocharge his organization's product development decisions to help maintain Intel's leadership position in a fiercely competitive industry.

These are ambitious goals, the kind that get people fired up—and each leader made it clear that better decision making and execution were essential to achieving them. If you have done the diagnoses described in chapter 2, you may have all the evidence you need to support the connection between effective decisions and your goals. When Broughton took over, for example, he found that only 5 percent of managers believed the company had a clear global strategy. More than 80 percent thought that strategic decisions weren't made quickly enough. Those and similar statistics created a dramatic burning platform. How could a company ever be number one with an organization that couldn't effectively make or communicate the decisions essential to good performance?

The rationale has to define success in big-picture terms—reaching strategic goals, turning in great results—because people may otherwise be tempted to think parochially. Consider UD Trucks, whose story we told in chapter 5. The company's shift to a national strategy made logical sense, but regional sales directors could easily have perceived the change as a loss of autonomy and regional side-by-side support. So the company had to help them embrace a common definition of success and understand what it would mean for them. This kind of alignment was one of the main goals of a two-day conference that brought all one hundred branch managers together to launch the new national sales company. The sales company's newly appointed president appeared on stage and asked all the managers to join hands. "You are not alone anymore," he said. "You are part of a network with one hundred branches. Even when you face difficulties, you can work with all the others." Linking the success of each branch to that of the company cut through the potential parochialism and made everyone feel part of a bigger whole.

Just knowing the reason for the journey isn't enough, of course: you have to broadcast it far and wide, preferably over and over again. Restate the connection between the organization's goals and better decisions. Remind everyone of the plan. Use whatever formats and media work best. MetLife's Henrikson, along with the company's chief investment officer and chief financial officer, videotaped a speech that was shown at leadership meetings throughout the company. The three officers declared that MetLife would become a "decision-driven organization." It would use best-practice tools to increase the speed of decisions and optimize the effort involved. MetLife, which had never relied on a single predominant style for major decisions, would now shift to a participative style, with all the changes in leadership behaviors that shift implied. All these measures, the officers said, would help the company become a true top performer. Leaders in each area of the business shared the video with their own teams and echoed the messages whenever they could. A year later, they were still starting major meetings with reminders of how important decision effectiveness was and what everyone still needed to do to improve it. Few could miss the fact that this was a high priority.

Align the top team and engage influential leaders early

People throughout the organization will be energized only if they see the top team aligned behind the effort and influential leaders throughout the business committed to change. Henrikson's urgent appeal to boost decision effectiveness, for example, found a receptive ear in Bill Mullaney, then head of MetLife's Institutional Business segment, which accounted for more than 40 percent of the company's earnings. Mullaney rallied his executive team and met with his top two hundred leaders to talk about why decision effectiveness was so important and to enlist their support. Then Maria Morris began to mobilize her team in Technology & Operations to work on decision effectiveness. Soon other leaders were following suit. Seeing influential executives like Mullaney and Morris embrace the effort was just the inspiration they needed.

We've found that two techniques are particularly helpful in engaging influential leaders, wherever those leaders might sit in the organization:

- *Build commitment through hands-on experience.* There's nothing like doing it yourself. If key players can see for themselves what these new approaches can accomplish, they're likely to speak honestly and passionately about the benefits of change. Doug Davis at Intel's Embedded and Communications Group (ECG) kicked off the decision focus with an offsite management meeting involving his top ten leaders. On the first day, Davis gave a presentation on how to think about using RAPID tools to flesh out deci-sion-making processes. Each member of the team then picked a handful of key decision areas and worked to define the RAPID roles associated with them. "My staff rolled up their sleeves; they got into it pretty deep," says Davis. "I think as they started seeing how the tool really worked, it was much easier for them to endorse it to their teams. And then, frankly, you had a bunch of people fairly quickly who had good understanding and were advocates."

- *Ask leaders to co-create the plan.* Especially where the level of change will be significant, key leaders must be involved in co-creating the new organization and the plan to build it. At BAT, Broughton picked people he knew would play central roles in the new organization, and he gave them responsibility for leading the redesign. Paul Adams, who became BAT's CEO in 2004, led the process in marketing, a critical area for the company. At MetLife, while rollout plans in each business and function had some common elements, leaders tailored the approach to the needs and challenges of their own areas.

Once the top team and other influential leaders are on board and engaged in the process, the job of spreading the new ideas and approaches to the rest of the company becomes that much easier. Decision effectiveness no longer seems like an edict from on high. It's something that can truly help people at every level to improve performance.

Creating and sustaining momentum

If you have successfully laid the foundation, actually setting out on the journey will spark enthusiasm. People will be curious about the new effort. They're likely to ask how they can get on board. Now the task is to harness that energy, build momentum, and begin to execute the plan.

Apply good decision disciplines to improving decision effectiveness itself

Want a practical demonstration of how decision effectiveness can make a difference? Take all the good decision practices described in this book and apply them to the process you will use to improve decision effectiveness. Establish clear accountabilities for the people who lead the effort. Define the roles involved in selecting and resetting decisions, and in redesigning elements of the organizational system. Clarify up front the what, who, how, and when for each of these major decisions. Manage the process one decision at a time, with a well-defined timetable. Use the appropriate decision style. If your organization needs to move away from consensus, for instance, run the process in a participative manner.

One key judgment call you'll have to make is what must be decided at higher levels and what can be pushed outward. Ultimately, responsibility for this kind of change effort can't be delegated. The senior leader—for a companywide effort, the CEO—has to be involved from the beginning and has to stay involved. He or she must make the tough calls on decision accountabilities, organizational redesign, and people changes. But plenty of other decisions can be delegated, especially since you want future leaders involved in the process. The trick is to determine what's negotiable and what isn't. If the whole organization is going to use RAPID, nobody can decide to opt out. If a global unit is assigned decision rights for a particular area, country organizations can't go off on their own. But not every issue requires a consistent approach. "You have to show some flexibility," says Lafarge's Gérard Kuperfarb. "Be firm on what you believe needs to be identical and what can be flexible. For example, not all aspects of our new model work for developing countries where we're building our presence. We've had to adapt to make it practical for them, but be clear what the path is to get back to the standard."

Remember, too, that this process isn't just about making decisions; it's about executing them. We like to give audiences a quiz about three frogs on a log. One frog decides to jump off; how many are left on the log? Though they know it's a trick question, listeners are often baffled. Some say two, the obvious choice; others say zero, figuring the first frog rocked the log and knocked the others off. But the answer is three, because deciding to do something isn't the same as doing it. This homely lesson applies doubly to the change effort: if you don't take action, the whole thing will peter out. We once observed a company that redesigned its organization to support decisions—and then the CEO took three months to begin implementing the plan. The effort was dead on arrival as a result. Some frustrated leaders left, and the company lost the opportunity to bring about the change it so badly needed.

MetLife was quite different. The company launched its decision effectiveness effort as part of a broader change management program called Operation Excellence. Once the decision effort was under way, the company appointed Bill Moore, head of its Auto & Home business, to lead the charge. Moore's job was to monitor progress, encourage and support the various businesses and functions, and ensure that the new decision approaches became part of how MetLife did business day to day.

Celebrate decision and execution successes—and nurture grassroots pull

While clear goals and hands-on involvement will help you make the necessary decisions and begin to execute the plan, you are

134 Decide & Deliver

likely to need more than that to get liftoff. People have to see evidence that the effort is worth it. They have to understand that there will be real victories. So announce the early wins loud and clear. Communicate them, celebrate them, show that others are likely to follow. Note that the early wins don't have to be huge. Hospira's success with the marketing materials may not have been an earth-shattering accomplishment, but it got people thinking that this kind of change could work, and it encouraged them to tackle other decisions. The effect was much the same with MetLife Auto & Home's new method for evaluating IT investment decisions. It delivered tangible, measurable improvements to the process and illustrated the possibilities of the new approach.

Of course, it's not just new decision methods that need to be celebrated; it's execution as well. David Fell, now BAT's director of Eastern Europe, recalls, "It really started to move when we started having some success in BAT Russia. We were becoming a unified organization, launching new brands as a single entity." Under Sol Trujillo, the Australian telecommunications company Telstra declared that it would build a new nationwide 3G wireless network in one year, a project that would ordinarily take three years. Employees believed the timetable was crazy—until they met it. The record-breaking launch had a significant impact on the culture. It showed the operations team what they were capable of delivering. It changed the perception of how quickly Telstra could act—which, says one observer, was "a lot better than all the road shows you could come up with on the new cultural values." Trujillo himself understood the impact. "When we became not just the industry leader in Australia but a global leader in wireless performance, it changed the whole culture of the business," he says. "It was a game-changing moment in time when you step from one culture to another."

One benefit of early wins is that they inspire people at the grassroots to explore the changes for their own organizations. Nothing is quite as powerful as when decision effectiveness goes viral—when people begin to say spontaneously, "I'd like to do that in my area," or "Where can I go to learn about this?" Yet that's often what happens once individuals get a whiff of early successes and hear how decisions are being unblocked and bureaucracy eradicated.

Nearly every successful adoption of new decision tools and approaches has been accelerated by this kind of viral take-up. At BAT, Martin Broughton launched "Golden Leaf" awards for teams that best lived up to the company's new ideals—and soon found that teams all over the world were actively competing to win. At Hospira, the organization used "Lunch and Learn" sessions to meet the demand for information about RAPID and decision X-ray tools. At another pharmaceutical company, where product development had launched a decision effectiveness effort, people in that function began to get calls from manufacturing and other areas asking how they could do the same. Davis at Intel learned about RAPID because it was being used in another part of the business—and his team now acts as ambassadors to other areas. "I started talking in my boss's staff meetings about what we were doing with RAPID and reporting back about the great results," says Davis, "because my peers were having the same kind of decision issues. And the more I talked about it, the more they started latching on to it, saying, 'Hey, we want to know more.' It started to spread pretty quickly."

So nurture this grassroots pull carefully. If you're a leader, think about how to generate more. If you're involved in a journey in your area, tell other people about the new approaches and how they're working for you. Soon you'll have a nearly unstoppable combination—committed leadership pushing for change and an active grassroots pulling the change into every nook and cranny of the organization.

Embedding decision behaviors and capabilities

A car's engine has to be turned over by a starter motor before it will engage. But once the gasoline ignites in the cylinders, the engine's operation becomes self-sustaining. In an organization, the challenge is to find similar ways of generating momentum to the point that the changes keep going and reinforce themselves. The following pages offer some tips for ensuring that decision-based behaviors become an intrinsic part of your organization.

Build new capabilities and skills

Improving decision making and execution requires investing in new skills and capabilities. Successful companies have developed four essential techniques for helping people handle important decisions more effectively.

- *Develop a repeatable model that can be applied throughout the business.* A repeatable formula helps ensure that people learn the same general tools and vocabulary, and that they can apply the tools to one decision after another. The model both defines and embeds the new capability. MetLife, for instance, established a step-by-step approach to decisions and codified a set of tools that made it easier for each business and function to apply best practices in its own area. So once an area had its scorecard results and decided to take the plunge, people went through much the same routine as in other areas—establishing the key decisions, deciding which ones to tackle, conducting decision X-rays and decision resets, and then installing the changes and measuring the effects. This repeatable approach meant that people could tackle a few decisions and improve them, tackle the next set, and so on, until the approach became a natural part of continuous improvement.

- *Use a "train the trainer" approach—and tailor the training to the audience.* Training trainers enables companies to teach the new approach to large numbers of people in a relatively short time. Intel, for example, trained more than six hundred managers in RAPID and other decision techniques through twenty-five workshops. These managers then trained another four thousand managers, and that group rolled RAPID out to many more thousands of people. Of course, not everyone needs the same content—it's better to identify specific segments of employees and adjust the training to their situations. At MetLife, senior leaders and designated rollout champions got directly involved in redesigning important decisions and discussing the leadership behaviors that would be critical to the change. The next tier of leaders—individuals who would lead efforts to improve decisions in their areas—attended half-day sessions that taught them how to evaluate and redesign individual decisions. People from this group then worked on specific decisions, with support from the senior team and rollout leaders. In addition, a one-hour e-learning program provided an overview of the approach, helping people in the broader organization understand key terms, expected behaviors, and the like.

- *Help people learn through experience.* Just as leaders need hands-on experience, so do other people throughout the organization. So the most successful training programs are designed around actual decisions, not just theoretical exercises. Teams work with experienced coaches to develop capabilities on the job rather than in the classroom. Hospira, for instance, started its training with a discussion of results from the decision and organizational scorecards. Participants then focused on real decisions drawn from their jobs. They spent most of their time actually applying the frameworks and tools rather than just hearing about them.

- *Share best practices.* Sharing best practices accelerates learning. Hospira named ten "Decision Champions" charged with working with business leaders to identify and improve key decisions and to share best practices along the way. At MetLife, executives held kickoff meetings in their own areas, inviting leaders from units that had already begun redesigning decisions to discuss their experiences.

Hearing both the positive elements and the challenges helped the new adopters understand what they were getting into. The company also formalized best-practice sharing by creating a council of rollout leaders from each area of the business. This council reviews progress, helps to resolve emerging issues, and collaborates on how best to track improvements in decision effectiveness.

At times, improving decision effectiveness may involve nurturing and developing other kinds of skills, such as creative thinking or financial analysis. U.K. retailer John Lewis improved its buying decisions by developing a "buyer's toolkit" and training buyers on matters such as product assortment, in-store presentations, and sourcing. HCL, the global IT and technology company, improved its performance on big contracts by more than 60 percent by creating a specialized team staffed by almost one hundred of its brightest engineers. The Dow Chemical Company coached people not only on how to track execution but also on how to develop contingency plans and take corrective action when needed. If a company's capability gap is too great, of course, it may need to hire people with the necessary skills or else tap outside expertise.

Walk the talk

Training people in the new skills is just a start; those individuals must then commit to actually using the new skills, even when it means changing long-standing ways of working. One big motivator for many people is seeing leaders act in new ways. MetLife, for instance, made a decision to consolidate its U.S. businesses into a single organizational unit. Once the decision was reached to form a new organization, the new president of that entity, Bill Mullaney, went through a process of designing the organizational structure. Shortly after the new structure was announced, the leadership team discussed where a certain part of the organization should report. Mullaney, with input from members of his team, determined that this particular function needed to move from one part of the organization to another in order to create better synergy and alignment. But rather than simply announcing the change, he sent an e-mail to every manager in the business explaining how his team had made the decision and why he felt it was a good one. He recounted how he had used some of the new decision practices he was trying to reinforce across the business— getting the right people in the room, considering alternatives, evaluating the options with the right facts, and communicating the decision with a well-defined rationale. In an example of the participative style, he had made the decision himself once he felt he had the right input, without striving for the consensus that would once have dragged the decision out. The message was crystal clear: this is the new way of doing things, and here's how it works.

Leaders at times face pivotal moments in their quest to improve decision effectiveness, and they have to seize those moments to reinforce the new behaviors. When Alan Mulally arrived at Ford, he created a plan for the company and a series of new measures that would assess progress against the plan. He then asked his team to begin producing color-coded charts showing their progress, with green indicating that things were on target and red indicating problem areas. When the first charts came in, everything was coded green. After several weeks of favorable reports, Mulally stopped a leadership team meeting by saying, "Friends, we lost $14 billion last year. And you're showing me that *everything* is going well?" The very next week, Mark Fields, president of Ford Americas, faced a critical setback in launching the company's new Edge crossover in Canada. At that week's business plan review, Fields brought in a chart with several indicators colored bright red. A hush fell over the group: what would Mulally do? Maybe Fields would get a tongue-lashing for his unit's misstep. Instead, Mulally began to clap. "That's great visibility, Mark," he said. "What can we all do to help you get back on track?" Mulally remembers that the next week, "the entire deck [of charts] looked like a rainbow. Because people had learned it was OK to report the truth." No doubt, those leaders brought the same message back to their own teams and found ways to drive the point home.[1]

Measure the impact

Any change effort, big or small, requires resources, time, and management attention. Naturally, you want to know whether you're getting a return on your investment. You need to know where you're seeing positive results so that you can let people know about them and build momentum for further progress. And if you're not making progress, of course, you need to know this as well, so that you can get things back on track. We have seen two types of measures work well to help improve decision effectiveness.

The first type tracks your overall progress. For instance, you can run the decision diagnostic and organizational health surveys again and compare scores. Have you moved up a quartile in decision effectiveness? Do people perceive that the organizational obstacles have been addressed? One tech company we worked with was so dismayed with its initial scores—it was in the bottom quartile—that it included moving up a quartile in its leadership objectives for the year, with part of executives' compensation tied to achieving that objective. Hospira has launched an annual employee engagement survey to track progress on quality, speed, yield, and effort, and to identify further areas for improvement. It has also developed a check-in for its biweekly senior leadership meeting. The check-in tracks three measures: what processes have changed, and how; which tasks have been eliminated as a result; and what new work has been added. It helps ensure that progress toward decision effectiveness is firmly rooted in Hospira's overall cost and effectiveness effort.

Another set of measurements tracks progress on the specific decisions that you are working to improve. You may be able to measure quality and speed directly: Davis's team at Intel, for example, created new metrics for each major-product decision process, tracking such indicators as number of decisions revisited, percentage of decision delays, meeting time dedicated to a decision, and so on. You can also survey people involved in specific decisions. What's their view of quality, speed, yield, and effort? Which organizational barriers have improved, and which have not? Short, quick decision X-rays can also help evaluate progress on specific decisions. The more you're able to measure, the greater the payoff you'll see, both in enthusiasm about achievements and in resolve to tackle the remaining challenges. Good measurement reinforces the need for continuous improvement.

Even if you follow all these prescriptions, the journey to decision effectiveness isn't necessarily an easy one. It takes determination and perseverance. Maria Morris got her leadership team committed to drive the change. Team members learned RAPID, decision X-rays, and other techniques. They laid out a plan, appointed a rollout leader, and worked with the organization to identify critical decisions and redesign them. By the end of 2009, Morris and her team had worked through nearly twenty major decisions, and the new approaches were starting to gain traction. Maybe most important, the organization was beginning to show signs of a culture change—people were learning to act differently, day in and day out. Though Morris was enthusiastic about the results so far, she would be the first to tell you that the journey was far from over.

Pitfalls to avoid

Nearly every effort to improve decisions encounters some obstacles. But many of these obstacles are predictable and can be avoided. Here are our recommendations for handling the four most common stumbling blocks.

Don't start anything you're not prepared to finish

There's no point in setting out on the road to decision effectiveness unless you plan to make the whole trip. If you start rallying the troops but don't follow through and don't make the necessary changes, cynicism sets in quickly. Nor should you declare victory too early. Improving a few decision processes doesn't mean you're done. In particular, don't shy away from the organizational changes that may be required to sustain decision effectiveness. "Make sure the organization's leaders are on top of this," advises Boys Town project leader Barb Vollmer in an interview with The Bridgespan Group. "If that's not the case, don't even begin. You would just create hope and then crush it. You would lose morale."

Plenty of organizations have fallen headfirst into this pothole. One technology company undertook a six-month project designed to improve decisions involving headquarters and its European team. When the project concluded that the company needed to delegate more decisions to Europe, headquarters nixed the whole effort. Within a year, many in the frustrated European team had moved on to other companies.

Apply the tools to the difficult decisions, not just the easy ones

While it's good to get some quick wins on simpler decisions, the real value of our process comes from tackling high-value decisions that are messy and complicated. RAPID helped Boys Town, for instance, deal with one of the toughest decisions any organization must face: which sites to close. "We closed three sites when we realized they didn't have the potential to help achieve our strategy, and we will reinvest those resources at other sites where we can help even more children," says Father Boes, the executive director. "Having a good plan and having the RAPID structure to push decision making to the right level made the decisions to close these sites and reinvest in others much easier."

Dow, too, applied these techniques to its big decisions. The acquisition of specialty chemical company Rohm and Haas is an example—the transaction carried many potential benefits but also entailed considerable risk. The team outlined its criteria, worked through alternatives, and ultimately made the tough decision to proceed. "That kind of decision making is now tied directly to the core fundamentals of our business," CEO Andrew Liveris told us. To be sure, big, one-off decisions like plant closings and acquisitions are not the only issues that need to be addressed with the new approaches. Everyday operational decisions can run into severe bottlenecks, especially when they cut across organizational boundaries. BAT, for instance, knew that the most value would come from wading into some particularly contentious areas, such as marketing. There, future CEO Paul Adams helped sort out the roles of the new global marketing function and local country marketers so that decisions in this critical realm worked more smoothly.

Don't fudge the people issues

Sometimes, everybody works hard to redesign decisions and change the organization—and meanwhile, the issue that dwarfs everything else is that the wrong person is in a key role. Tom Farrell of Lafarge recalls needing to confront just this kind of issue in transforming the aggregates business. "One of our business unit managers wasn't able to adapt to the new way of working. We knew he was close to retirement, so we delayed implementation for a few months, when we could move much more quickly." Of course, you may need to take more decisive action, either redeploying people or letting them go. At BAT, some of the senior executives couldn't or wouldn't embrace the new approach. Top leaders gave them time to adjust, but ultimately realized that these executives had to leave the business if they were unable to change. In general, says Lafarge's Kuperfarb, "You push gently at first, then less gently. You set targets that they can't achieve without changing. Maybe you have to let some people go."

Cut bureaucracy—don't add to it

Focus your efforts on the decisions that matter most, not on every decision. The goal is not to have binders of RAPID charts and process maps gathering dust on shelves. A true test of success, one client says, is to do the RAPID assignments and the other fixes we describe, imprint the new way of working so that behaviors really change, and then throw out the rulebook. Something like that is just what happened at Intel's ECG. "Four to six months into it," says Davis, "I was starting to get questions—'How far do you want to take this?'—and jokes, such as 'Do you realize we're doing a RAPID on who's going to buy sandwiches for the meeting?' As the novelty wore off, things settled out at the right level." The lesson: invest in applying best practices to your most important decisions, with the twin goals of improving those decisions and making the approach intuitive for many other decisions.

Like potholes on a highway, any of these traps can interrupt your journey. If you avoid them, you'll be better able to speed on your way.

ABB's journey

We began this book with the story of Trevor Gregory and ABB, and we described in brief how ABB resolved its problems. But the whole thing took time, and along the way, the company followed many of the approaches outlined in this chapter.

Take our stricture about making decision effectiveness a priority. No one at ABB could miss the fact that the company was changing the way it made and executed decisions. Every employee got a weekly e-mail from the CEO talking about the transformation— what the priorities were, what the challenges were, how the company was doing. The five members of the executive team distributed a video explaining the core elements, and of course each member of the team spent a huge amount of time out rallying the troops. "It meant tremendous traveling, I can tell you," remembers Dinesh Paliwal, then head of the Automation Technologies division. "I was out seventy-five percent of the time, holding town-hall meetings and business reviews, and of course at the same time visiting as many clients as I could."

ABB also engaged influential leaders who worked jointly to create solutions. Some of the task forces charged with designing the new ABB, for instance, involved not just executive committee members but future committee members and senior country managers from around the world. In Paliwal's division, he remembers,

"I would say to my team, 'I don't have all the answers, but if you guys don't come up with great ideas, I will tell you my great ideas. So if you don't want to hear my ideas all the time, you give me yours. And we'll pick the best of them.' "

And so it went. ABB didn't shrink from difficult decisions, whether they were about divesting noncore or unprofitable businesses or about investing in key growth priorities such as R&D and China. It celebrated early wins and encouraged grassroots pull. A cost-cutting program known as StepChange, for instance, was deliberately designed to generate an early win—and it did, saving the company more than $1 billion. "I think it was the first cost-reduction program that ABB had ever delivered on time and on budget," says Gary Steel with a laugh. "But it was a fundamental part of the culture change. If you can teach people to think differently about the money they spend, the chances are they'll make better decisions."

The leadership walked the talk relentlessly. It started with then-CEO Jürgen Dormann, who set a new style for decisions and action. "Jürgen talked in his weekly letters about his style," recalls Stephan Volker, an HR executive, about what the CEO expected of himself and others: to take accountability, to do the right thing for the company, and to make and execute the tough decisions necessary to drive the transformation. Bernhard Jucker, head of ABB's Power Products Division and group executive committee member, adds, "We were working along a tight timeline with clearly defined trigger points. We openly discussed and prioritized the issues, agreed on actions, and implemented them swiftly." The days of parochialism and politics were over. People saw their leaders making and executing decisions and dealing with one another with cohesion and trust. "It started to build like a wave," says Tarak Mehta, now head of ABB's Global Transformers business. "It was one quarter after another of delivering what we promised and exceeding external expectations."

It is challenging to achieve and sustain the kind of change that took place at ABB and the other companies we have described. No single change turns a company into the kind of organization that is capable of making good decisions and executing them again and again. No organization can provide for all the contingencies and business shifts that a company is bound to encounter along the way. The most successful companies take an integrated approach, as we have described, but they also pick their spots. They understand that change is a journey, not a one-step process. They begin by tackling whichever aspect of their organization has the greatest potential for impact. They continue to improve, adjusting as their business responds to new opportunities. They work to enhance their decision capabilities across the organization, from the boardroom to the front line.

But once an organization begins to hum, once it learns to decide and deliver, the effect is dramatic. If it's a company, it's the one that stands out in its industry, the one everyone wants to be part of. If it's a smaller organization or part of a larger one, it's the one with the reputation that everyone hears about. If you don't know what's behind the change, the improvements can seem like magic. But there's no magic to it, only discipline, commitment, and a relentless focus on decisions. When organizations adopt that focus, they can and do improve. They get things done. They create the kind of environment where people look forward to coming to work because they know that they have the mandate and the capabilities to decide and deliver.

Your organization can be like this. It can be the standout, the one that people point to, the one where everyone wants to work, the one that decides and delivers. Your organization can accomplish great things—beginning with its next decision.

The Research Behind
Decide & Deliver

THIS BOOK IS SUPPORTED BY DATA and analysis from executive interviews, quantitative field research, prior studies, and publicly available sources. This appendix summarizes the studies and methods.

Interviews

Purpose: To gather wisdom, advice, and lessons learned from executives and managers who have helped their organizations improve decision effectiveness.

Methodology: We identified companies in many industries and countries that had successfully improved decision effectiveness or were well on the way to doing so. Within each company, we interviewed executives and managers from various levels of the organization, asking for their perspectives on the change. Many of these individuals had experienced the difficulties of dysfunctional systems and structures. Most of the leaders played a key role in helping to transform their organizations. The full list of interviewees follows:

- ABB

  - Trevor Gregory, managing director, ABB UK

  - Bernhard Jucker, head of power products and member of the group executive committee

  - Tarak Mehta, vice president of operations, high-voltage products

  - Dinesh Paliwal, chairman and CEO, Harman International; former president of global markets and technology, ABB

  - Gary Steel, head of human resources and member of the group executive committee

  - Stephan Volker, group senior vice president, human resources development

- British American Tobacco (BAT)

  - Paul Adams, CEO

  - Martin Broughton, former chairman

  - David Crow, director of Australasia

  - David Fell, director of Eastern Europe

- Cardinal Health

  - Bob Walter, chairman

- DaVita

  - Kent Thiry, chairman and CEO

- Diageo

  - Gareth Williams, human resources director

- The Dow Chemical Company

  - Andrew Liveris, CEO

- Ford Motor Company

  - Lewis Booth, executive vice president and chief financial officer

  - Fergus Jamieson, former brand development manager

  - Alan Mulally, CEO

- Hospira

  - Ken Meyers, senior vice president, organizational transformation and people development

  - Kim Pope, director, human resources, global marketing and corporate development and organization effectiveness

- Intel

  - Doug Davis, vice president of the Intel architecture group; general manager of the Embedded and Communications Group

- Lafarge

  - Tom Farrell, executive vice president and copresident, Aggregates & Concrete Division

  - Gérard Kuperfarb, executive vice president and copresident, Aggregates & Concrete Division

  - Sara Ravella, senior vice president, communications

- UD Trucks

  - Koji Sakurai, vice president

- Shinhan Bank

  - Baek Soon Lee, president and CEO, Shinhan Bank

- Sang Hoon Shin, CEO, Shinhan Financial Group

- Sung Ho Wi, deputy president, Shinhan Financial Group

• Telstra

- Gavan Corcoran, executive director

- Andrea Grant, group managing director, human resources

- Glenice Maclellan, former acting group managing director, consumer and channels

- Sol Trujillo, former CEO

• Unilever

- Sandy Ogg, chief human resources director

• United Kingdom National Health Service

- Clare Chapman, director general; former group personnel director, Tesco

• Vodafone

- Chris Gent, former CEO and chairman

- Phil Williams, former group director, human resources

Quantitative field research

Purpose: To test whether our experience with decision effectiveness and organizational health was supported by statistical analysis of a large population of companies from a wide range of industries and geographic locations.

The three concepts we tested are these:

• Decision effectiveness can be defined and measured

• Decision effectiveness is correlated with financial results

- Organizational health is correlated with decision effectiveness

Methodology and database. We tested the connections between organizational health, decision effectiveness, and financial results by surveying 760 companies on these topics. The survey and database, completed in July 2008, were developed with support from eRewards, a market research specialist.

Most of the 760 companies were headquartered in the United States, United Kingdom, Germany, France, China, and Japan. Our sample included most industry groups, including airlines, consumer products, retail, financial services, health care, manufacturing, professional services, technology, and telecommunications. The companies varied in size from $500 million to more than $50 billion in annual revenue. The respondents came from every managerial level, from the C-suite to frontline supervisors.

The survey included eighty-five questions divided into five sections:

- Demographic information and financial performance

- Decision effectiveness—quality, speed, yield, and effort

- Organizational health—structure, roles, processes, information, measures and incentives, priorities, decision style, people, behaviors, and culture

- Decision obstacles

- Employee engagement as measured by Net Promoter® Score (NPS®)

Most questions offered four possible answers representing the degree to which respondents agreed or disagreed with a particular statement. For example, "Please use a scale from 1 (strongly disagree) to 4 (strongly agree) to respond to the following statement: We have specific and measurable corporate goals."

Because the survey was administered anonymously, we tracked financial returns through two separate channels. First, we asked the 760 respondents to provide an assessment of their organizations' financial performance in terms of quintiles. This was incorporated into their self-reported financial performance score. Second, we asked each respondent to volunteer the name of his or her company. For those who provided this information, we used standard databases to gather actual financial returns for the period 2001–2006. We also tested the relationship between self-reported financial performance and actual financial returns for the data set where we had both. We found that self-reported financial performance can be used as a statistically valid proxy. Total shareholder returns, for example, correlate with self-reported performance at a 97 percent confidence level.

Decision effectiveness can be defined and measured. To determine the best measure of decision effectiveness and to understand its implications, we performed five separate analyses.

First, we defined four components of decision effectiveness. Our experience had persuaded us that decision effectiveness is not just about making good decisions; it also requires speed, execution, and the right amount of effort. To understand how companies performed on each of these components, we asked them to consider their most important strategic and operational decisions over the previous three years and rate them on questions such as the following:

- *Quality:* Given the benefit of hindsight, how often does your organization choose the right course of action?

- *Speed:* How quickly is your organization able to make decisions—faster than competitors, slower, or about the same?

- *Yield:* How often does your organization execute decisions as intended?

- *Effort:* How much effort does your organization put into making and executing decisions—more than it should, less than it should, or about the right amount?

Second, we built an overall measure of decision effectiveness that matched our experience. The measure highlights the multiplicative effect of strength in each of the areas. We used the following formula to score each company's decision effectiveness:

Decision score = Quality × Speed × Yield − Effort

We then identified the top quintile of companies and compared their performance with the rest of our sample. We found that on average, the top quintile excelled at all four of the attributes. Specifically, this group made 38 percent better decisions (quality), made them 37 percent faster (speed), executed them 38 percent more effectively (yield), and were 2.7 times as likely to use the right amount of effort in the process.

Third, we used statistical techniques to assess the importance of each component to each company's overall decision effectiveness and to its financial performance. The findings were similar: quality, speed, and yield have similarly high correlations with decision effectiveness and financial performance, though speed is slightly higher and quality is slightly lower. Effort has a lower, but still significant, impact. Companies' overall decision score as produced by the formula correlated better with their financial results than did their score on any single element.

Fourth, we investigated the commonly held belief that the different elements of decision effectiveness trade off with one another. Are slower decisions better decisions? Are the best decisions more difficult to implement? We found that these conventional ideas are not supported by the data. Only 8 percent of our respondents showed significant trade-offs between quality, speed, and yield. In fact, the companies that made the fastest decisions were 4.2 times as likely to make the best decisions, and the companies that made the best decisions were 8.2 times as likely to excel at execution compared with the rest of the companies in the sample. While Japanese companies, like others, showed high correlations between decision effectiveness and financial performance, they also showed the highest level of trade-offs: some 26 percent of Japanese companies scored high on either speed or quality but not both. Of that group, almost two-thirds indicated that they have slow but high-quality decisions, and a similar percentage said they had slow but well-executed decisions. Our data on Japan, unlike the rest of our data, seems to bear out the common wisdom about trade-offs.

Finally, we quantified the headroom most companies have to improve decision effectiveness. What level of improvement is available to an organization trying to boost its performance on these dimensions? Our findings matched our experience. The highest possible score using our formula is 100. The top quintile of companies averaged 71, and the remaining companies averaged 28. Consequently, average companies in the bottom four quintiles could realistically strive for gains of between 2.5 and 3.5 times their current decision effectiveness. This is a substantial incentive to get it right.

Decision effectiveness is correlated with financial results. To understand the link between decision effectiveness and financial returns, we compared various financial performance measures of top-quintile companies against the rest of our sample. The results were compelling.

First, we compared the companies' actual total shareholder return and found that top-quintile companies earned their shareholders on average almost 6 percentage points more per year than did other companies. Next, we examined revenue growth. The top-quintile grew revenues by 5 percentage points more per year on average than the rest of our sample did. We also looked at return on invested capital (ROIC) and found that the top quintile generated an average ROIC 6 percentage points higher than that produced by the remaining quintiles.

As a final check, we compared each company's decision effectiveness with its self-reported financial performance. True to form, our best companies were 3.4 times as likely to rate themselves "excellent" in terms of financial performance. Of course, these relationships describe correlations and do not demonstrate causation. Nor do our statistical observations specify the direction of the relationship—that is, we cannot say whether decision effectiveness drives financial performance or vice versa. However, our experience with hundreds of companies over many years gives us confidence that improvements in decision effectiveness will produce better financial results.

Importantly, we recognize that some of our measures of decision effectiveness are based on self-reported assessments. So our findings could be subject to a "halo effect," meaning that individuals who work for companies with strong financial results, for example, ascribe better performance to their organizations in other areas, such as decisions. We found, however, that most companies didn't score uniformly well on all four elements of decision effectiveness—quite different from what we would have expected had the halo effect been significant. Also, whenever possible, we asked both subjective and objective questions to assess quality, speed, yield, and effort. We found that when objective measures were used—for example, the number of decisions made in a year—our statistical correlations were just as strong. While we cannot completely eliminate the potential halo effect in our results, we made every effort to minimize it.

Organizational health is correlated with decision effectiveness. Over the past eight years, we have developed a holistic model of organizational health. Through our experience, we have identified the ten elements of successful organizations:

- Structure
- Roles
- Processes
- Information
- Measures and incentives

- Priorities
- Decision style
- People
- Behaviors
- Culture

Earlier Bain studies have confirmed that all of these elements are critical to a high-performance organization. But to what extent do they influence an organization's decision effectiveness? To understand the connection between organizational health and decision effectiveness, we performed two key pieces of analysis.

First, we identified the elements of organizational health that are most important to decision effectiveness. We used statistical analyses to test the importance of each element. The results showed that all ten organizational elements are required for decision effectiveness. The softer elements, such as culture, behaviors, and people, actually have a somewhat stronger influence than the harder elements of structure, roles, and processes. This is consistent with our experience, which suggests that companies must move beyond organizational mechanics to register significant improvements in decision effectiveness.

Second, we attempted to determine whether specific organizational elements were associated with particular components of decision effectiveness—quality, speed, yield, and effort. If there were strong one-to-one relationships, leaders could focus on specific changes in their organizations to remedy specific decision shortcomings. For example, if companies had a speed problem, unclear roles might turn up as the primary cause. Unfortunately, there seemed to be no such one-to-one links. This supports our view that a healthy organizational system is required for strong performance. Companies that focus on just one or two elements of their organization do so at their peril.

Our key lessons hold across all geographic areas, industries, and company sizes. Over the past twenty years, we have worked with hundreds of companies facing these issues. We knew that the overall relationship between organizational health, decision effectiveness, and financial performance was likely to be strong. But one of the benefits of a wide-ranging research survey is the ability to look at specific environments to understand how the lessons might differ from one market to another. After analyzing the data to test our hypotheses at each managerial level, on each individual industry, in each country, and for each size of company, we found little difference in the overall correlations. Organizational health was highly correlated with decision effectiveness, and decision effectiveness was highly correlated with financial performance in every subset of the population we surveyed. The lessons in this book can be used by managers and leaders everywhere.

Prior research

Purpose: To leverage insights from prior research and publications by the authors.

Methodology: We reviewed the research and insights in four *Harvard Business Review* articles previously published by members of the author team to ensure that *Decide & Deliver* included as much of our collective experience as possible:

- "Stop Wasting Valuable Time," by Michael C. Mankins, September 2004

- "Turning Great Strategy into Great Performance," by Michael C. Mankins and Richard Steele, July–August 2005

- "Stop Making Plans, Start Making Decisions," by Michael C. Mankins and Richard Steele, January 2006

- "Who Has the D?" by Paul Rogers and Marcia Blenko, January 2006

Research from publicly available sources

Purpose: To gather specific demographic data and information (financial returns, ownership structure, location of headquarters, industry, and size of revenues) on the companies in our market research.

Methodology: We relied on multiple sources to fill in gaps, particularly where respondents had not provided enough information. These sources included the following:

- Worldscope and Datastream financial databases to gather total shareholder returns, revenues, and ROIC

- OneSource and annual reports to identify ownership, location of headquarters, and industry

- Company Web sites to find strategic and organizational changes that had dramatic impacts on decision effectiveness

- Literature reviews to understand what others' research and materials had revealed about decisions and organizations

- Previous Bain experience to identify key trends and challenges within decision and organizational effectiveness

- Various public surveys and other research (employee satisfaction, talent acquisition, human capital, meeting effectiveness, etc.) to review current figures and issues in organizations

NOTES

CHAPTER 1

1. Tom Peters, *Liberation Management* (New York: Alfred A. Knopf, 1992), 44.

2. Larry Bossidy and Ram Charan, *Execution: The Discipline of Getting Things Done* (New York: Crown Business, 2002).

3. Malcolm Gladwell, *Blink: The Power of Thinking Without Thinking* (New York: Little, Brown and Co., 2005); Dan Ariely, *Predictably Irrational: The Hidden Forces That Shape Our Decisions* (New York: Harper, 2008).

4. Thomas H. Davenport and Jeanne G. Harris, *Competing on Analytics: The New Science of Winning* (Boston: Harvard Business School Press, 2007).

5. James Surowiecki, *The Wisdom of Crowds: Why the Many Are Smarter Than the Few and How Collective Wisdom Shapes Business, Economies, Societies, and Nations* (New York: Doubleday, 2004).

CHAPTER 2

1. Andrew Edgecliffe-Johnson, "Levin Apologises for 'Worst Deal of Century,'" *Financial Times*, January 4, 2010.

2. "Fastest Drug Developers Consistently Best Peers on Key Performance Metrics," *Tufts Center for the Study of Drug Development Impact Report* 8, no. 5 (September/October 2006): 1.

CHAPTER 4

1. For a more detailed discussion, see Paul Rogers and Marcia Blenko, "Who Has the D? How Clear Decision Roles Enhance Organizational Performance," *Harvard Business Review*, January 2006.

2. Jon Huggett and Kirk Kramer, "Boys Town: Clarifying Decision-Making Roles Between Headquarters and Sites" (Boston: The Bridgespan Group, Inc., November 2008).

3. Michael C. Mankins, "Stop Wasting Valuable Time," *Harvard Business Review*, September 2004.

4. Ibid.

5. Cadbury has since been acquired by Kraft Foods.

CHAPTER 5

1. Darrell K. Rigby, *Management Tools 2009: An Executive's Guide* (Boston: Bain & Company, 2008).

2. Jon Huggett and Kirk Kramer, "Boys Town: Clarifying Decision-Making Roles Between Headquarters and Sites" (Boston: The Bridgespan Group, Inc., November 2008).

3. Michael C. Mankins and Richard Steele, "Stop Making Plans, Start Making Decisions," *Harvard Business Review*, January 2006.

4. See Michael C. Mankins, "Stop Wasting Valuable Time," *Harvard Business Review*, September 2004.

5. Ibid.

CHAPTER 6

1. This account is based on our own interviews and on reporting by Alex Taylor III of *Fortune* magazine. See "Fixing Up Ford," *Fortune*, May 11, 2009.

INDEX

ABOUT THE AUTHORS

Marcia W. Blenko (marcia.blenko@bain.com) leads Bain's Global Organization practice. She has extensive experience in decision effectiveness and organization design across a range of sectors. Marcia has authored numerous articles on organization, decision effectiveness, and leadership and often speaks on these topics. Her writings have appeared in *Harvard Business Review, Financial Times, Wall Street Journal, Economic Times, European Business Journal, Harvard Management Update*, and the World Economic Forum's *Global Agenda*. She is also a contributing author of *Winning in Turbulence* (Harvard Business Press, 2009). Marcia is a partner in Bain's Boston office.

Michael C. Mankins (michael.mankins@bain.com) leads Bain's Organization practice in the Americas and is a key member of Bain's Strategy practice. He advises business leaders on the strategic and organizational initiatives required to drive performance and long-term value. Michael's writings have appeared in *Harvard Business Review, Wall Street Journal, Financial Times, Harvard Management Update, Journal of Business Strategy, Directors & Boards, Chief Executive*, and other publications. He has been a featured speaker at numerous conferences and is coauthor of *The Value Imperative: Managing for Superior Shareholder Returns* (Free Press, 1994). In 2006, *Consulting* magazine named Michael one of the year's "top 25 most influential consultants." Michael is a partner in Bain's San Francisco office.

Paul Rogers (paul.rogers@bain.com) is the managing partner for Bain's London office and previously led Bain's Global Organization practice. Paul's organizational experience spans comprehensive transformation, decision effectiveness, culture change, talent management, front-line employee loyalty, overhead optimization, and change management. Paul has authored numerous articles on organizational effectiveness and successful change in *Harvard Business Review, European Business Forum, Business Strategy Series, Financial Times,* and others, and he regularly speaks on these topics.